US NAVY/CHRIS ROYS

USNS Alan Shephard

THE UNITED STATES NAVY

This new edition of our regular update on the state and composition of the US Navy, its auxiliaries and the US Coast Guard has seen a number of significant changes since the last edition, not least a new editor. The US Navy has continued to be the pre-eminent naval power in the world, although this status has been challenged, if not outright threatened, by the emerging blue water threat posed by China and the re-emergence of the Russian Bear after many years slumbering and has now truly re-awoken and poses a grave threat to the established naval supremacy of the American fleet.

2019 and beyond could pose threats both foreign and domestic for the US Navy. Republican Presidency's usually bode well for the American military but few Presidents in the past have been as erratic and cavalier as President Donald J. Trump has been since his election success. He both gives and takes with both hands and whilst seemingly fully supportive of the military has yet to deliver on his promises of more, more and more for the Air Force, Army, Marines and Navy, yet seemingly has money to spare to develop a fifth arm of the military spectrum namely the Space Defense Division. For the US Navy Trump has promised a 355-ship strong fleet, and 355 ships does not include small support vessels such as the LCS or anything smaller. Having 355 warships doesn't necessarily mean top of the line, technologically advanced front line warfighting capable ships. This would be a challenge for any President to force through and not since his Republican predecessor, and some may say equally erratic, Ronald Reagan has the military been bolstered by promises of more to come.

So where exactly is the US Navy in 2019 and what is in store for the next five, ten or twenty years into the future?

Technology is at the heart of modern warfare and technology of this complexity does not come cheap. At a recent Surface Navy Association annual symposium much of the talk was of robot technology. We have seen the first examples of robot warfare in the drones that patrol the skies over battlefields that can rain down a creditable punch in a timely and precise attack. They also add eyes and ears in the skies, and increasingly underwater too. More information and data is what war planners the world over crave. They feed on it and make better, well-informed decisions based on a wealth of sensors across the battlespace. When these sensors are distributed and networked it is a formidable weapon system in its own right and this linkage between assets large and small will play an increasingly important part in US Naval Strategy into the middle of the 21st century. One thing we have yet to see, however, is unmanned naval surface vessels, but in the next five to ten years new, reliable technology will make these vessels possible. Whilst robot warships will not be cheap, they are considerably less expensive than building a fleet of Arleigh Burke-class guided missile destroyers and crucially take out the human factor from the battlespace. Robots are expendable in military thinking, humans much less so. Currently the US Navy is trialling the Sea Hunter drone developed by DARPA (Defense Advanced Research Projects Agency).

There will always be a role for manned warships in a modern fleet, at least in the foreseeable future anyway and new designs are being formulated to satisfy a number of different roles across the US fleet. One of the most pressing is for the design and construction of the future frigate or FFG(X). With the passing of the last of the legacy FFG 7 Oliver Hazard Perry-class frigates from service the role of convoy escort, force multiplier and anti-submarine warfare has been pushed back into the long grass somewhat. This policy was, in part, allowed to happen due to the Soviet threat falling away following the collapse of the Soviet Union and its immense submarine fleet of the Cold War rusting away at their berths. The Russian Navy, however, has re-awoken and the growth of their fleet in a few short years has been staggering. With Vladamir Putin in command, Russia has signalled to the world it is ready and able to push its foreign policy agenda forward and to use military force to achieve it as it did with the annexation of the Crimea. Submarine construction has been accelerated in Russia but in the Western World it has declined significantly meaning there is a capability gap between the emerging new Russian submarines and the West's ability to detect and attack them. This is where the FFG(X) project will be thrust. In 2019 the US Navy expects to announce its requirements for the future frigate and seek tenders for the construction of the first of class sometime in 2020. Many expect the design to be based on the successful Coast Guard Maritime Security Cutter or Bertholf Class. At least twenty frigates are required to satisfy the need, perhaps even more.

Training and retention of trained personnel is a problem being faced by every nation and the United States is no exception. In 2019 the US Navy spent US$24 million to establish a Maritime Skills Training Program that relies heavily on the use of simulators to train the sailors of tomorrow. The centers will be ready to deliver their first qualified sailors back to the fleet in around 2021.

For the surface fleet 2019 will see the first Zumwalt-class ship. USS ZUMWALT entered service within the fleet following extensive sea trials. She, together with her two sister ships, will then be integrated into the fleet. The trio of ships are unique and offer the US Navy a fabulous opportunity to lead the world with each ship's massive surface strike capability. US Navy commanders welcome their arrival as they witness the cruisers of the Ticonderoga Class begin to wear out. These venerable ships are, currently, the most potent surface vessels besides the aircraft carriers, but they are old, dating back to the late 1970s. Their replacement is imperative and in 2019 we expect to hear more about the Large Surface Combatant program that will ultimately replace them in service, but the first new cruiser will probably not be ordered until 2024.

Aircraft carriers are the most visible and potent surface asset owned by the US Navy. They boast an air force comparable to some small nation's entire fleet and the United

States can lay claim to eleven flat tops. These massively impressive vessels, however, come with an astronomical price tag and many strategists fear their vulnerability in an age of technology. The Chinese Navy has frequently claimed its DF-26 Anti Ship Ballistic Missile could easily destroy an American aircraft carrier and the DF-26 is not the only weapon system that is ranged against the American fleet. Russia has been developing its own hypersonic missiles that could conceivably punch through last ditch defences and kill a carrier.

The American aircraft carrier despite all its enemies, is still an amazing visual representation of awe inspiring military might. Up to 90 aircraft can be stowed within a Nimitz-class ship and a similar number within the new Gerald R. Ford-class ships. Construction of the latter ships has started to gather pace with work well advanced on the second of the class USS JOHN F. KENNEDY and advanced items for the third USS ENTERPRISE in hand. The USS GERALD R. FORD has now, after many months of trials of its new EMALS launch system, started to enter operational service and relieve a rather tired force of ships. The oldest aircraft carrier USS NIMITZ entered service in 1976 and is expected to be replaced in service by the future USS JOHN F. KENNEDY; but that is still almost five years hence.

The US Navy is facing a capability and numbers time bomb with its submarine fleet. Large numbers of Los Angeles-class attack submarines are reaching the end of their service lives in greater numbers than their replacements are coming into service. To maintain the current level of submarines in service will require additional orders in the next few years; but even with those in place the level will fall in real terms despite President Trump's assertions of building the US Navy's strike capability.

Alongside the attack submarine force similar ageing problems face the Ohio-class nuclear ballistic missile force. These venerable submarines all date from the 1980s and early 1990s and whilst the future Columbia-class design is well in hand it will still be many years before the first of class enters service. Construction of the first submarine is expected to commence sometime in 2021. With submarine construction limited to just two shipyards at Newport News and Connecticut, shipbuilding capacity may not be sufficient to deliver the necessary numbers in the required time frame.

The US Navy's amphibious force has in the last twenty years received a great deal of funding and this has resulted in a fleet of modern amphibious warships that is the envy of many nations. Top of the tier are the flat tops of the Wasp and America class capable of delivering fully equipped force ashore by landing craft and helicopters and with their own organic air cover provided by Harrier jump jets and increasingly the new F-35 Lightning II as well as powerfully armed attack helicopters such as the Super Cobra Viper. The US Navy's stated aim is to have a 13:13:13 ratio of LHD/LPD/LSD and they are well on their way to achieving this ambitious target. The older Whidbey Island/Harper Valley-class LSD delivered between 1985 and 1998 are next in line for replacement and plans are advanced in this regard with a design based on the San Antonio-class LPD leading the field.

The US Navy has a number of challenges to face up to in the next few years. Training and retention of the best personnel is crucial and the Navy will need to show that it offers clear career paths for the most gifted young people. The fleet is also ageing, most notably with its aircraft carriers and submarine fleets. These ships take a great deal of money to maintain and to procure new ships is a laborious and extremely expensive process that can take decades to achieve. The US Navy has always set ambitious shipbuilding targets and with President Trump's call for an expansion of the fleet to 355 or even higher there is a possibility that the support system for the fleet including the shipyards dotted around the nation will find it impossible to cope with the demands placed on it. Added to this are international pressures posed by North Korea, the Middle East and not least China and the re-emergence of the threat of peer to peer conflict with Russia.

Patrick Boniface
Editorial Correspondent *Warship World*
April 2019

The Author: Patrick Boniface

Patrick Boniface is a journalist and broadcaster with over thirty years experience of writing for a range of naval and military magazines and journals. He has also written a number of books on naval subjects. Patrick is also a local radio broadcaster having worked on a number of stations in his home county of Kent, where he still lives.

SHIPS OF THE UNITED STATES NAVY
Hull Numbers

Ship	Hull Number	Ship	Hull Number
Aircraft Carriers		HENRY M. JACKSON	SSBN 730
		ALABAMA	SSBN 731
NIMITZ	CVN 68	ALASKA	SSBN 732
DWIGHT D. EISENHOWER	CVN 69	NEVADA	SSBN 733
CARL VINSON	CVN 70	TENNESSEE	SSBN 734
THEODORE ROOSEVELT	CVN 71	PENNSYLVANIA	SSBN 735
ABRAHAM LINCOLN	CVN 72	WEST VIRGINIA	SSBN 736
GEORGE WASHINGTON	CVN 73	KENTUCKY	SSBN 737
JOHN C. STENNIS	CVN 74	MARYLAND	SSBN 738
HARRY S. TRUMAN	CVN 75	NEBRASKA	SSBN 739
RONALD REAGAN	CVN 76	RHODE ISLAND	SSBN 740
GEORGE H.W. BUSH	CVN 77	MAINE	SSBN 741
GERALD R. FORD	CVN 78	WYOMING	SSBN 742
JOHN F. KENNEDY	CVN 79	LOUISIANA	SSBN 743
ENTERPRISE	CVN 80		
Unnamed	CVN 81	NEWPORT NEWS	SSN 750
Unnamed	CVN 82	SAN JUAN	SSN 751
		PASADENA	SSN 752
Submarines		ALBANY	SSN 753
		TOPEKA	SSN 754
SEAWOLF	SSN 21	SCRANTON	SSN 756
CONNECTICUT	SSN 22	ALEXANDRIA	SSN 757
JIMMY CARTER	SSN 23	ASHEVILLE	SSN 758
OLYMPIA	SSN 717	JEFFERSON CITY	SSN 759
PROVIDENCE	SSN 719	ANNAPOLIS	SSN 760
PITTSBURGH	SSN 720	SPRINGFIELD	SSN 761
CHICAGO	SSN 721	COLUMBUS	SSN 762
KEY WEST	SSN 722	SANTA FE	SSN 763
OKLAHOMA CITY	SSN 723	BOISE	SSN 764
LOUISVILLE	SSN 724	MONTPELIER	SSN 765
HELENA	SSN 725	CHARLOTTE	SSN 766
		HAMPTON	SSN 767
OHIO	SSGN 726	HARTFORD	SSN 768
MICHIGAN	SSGN 727	TOLEDO	SSN 769
FLORIDA	SSGN 728	TUCSON	SSN 770
GEORGIA	SSGN 729	COLUMBIA	SSN 771

Ship	Hull Number	Ship	Hull Number
GREENEVILLE	SSN 772	Unnamed	SSN 810
CHEYENNE	SSN 773	Unnamed	SSN 811
VIRGINIA	SSN 774		
TEXAS	SSN 775	**Cruisers**	
HAWAII	SSN 776		
NORTH CAROLINA	SSN 777	BUNKER HILL	CG 52
NEW HAMPSHIRE	SSN 778	MOBILE BAY	CG 53
NEW MEXICO	SSN 779	ANTIETAM	CG 54
MISSOURI	SSN 780	LEYTE GULF	CG 55
CALIFORNIA	SSN 781	SAN JACINTO	CG 56
MISSISSIPPI	SSN 782	LAKE CHAMPLAIN	CG 57
MINNESOTA	SSN 783	PHILIPPINE SEA	CG 58
NORTH DAKOTA	SSN 784	PRINCETON	CG 59
JOHN WARNER	SSN 785	NORMANDY	CG 60
ILLINOIS	SSN 786	MONTEREY	CG 61
WASHINGTON	SSN 787	CHANCELLORSVILLE	CG 62
COLORADO	SSN 788	COWPENS	CG 63
INDIANA	SSN 789	GETTYSBURG	CG 64
SOUTH DAKOTA	SSN 790	CHOSIN	CG 65
DELAWARE	SSN 791	HUE CITY	CG 66
VERMONT	SSN 792	SHILOH	CG 67
OREGON	SSN 793	ANZIO	CG 68
MONTANA	SSN 794	VICKSBURG	CG 69
HYMAN G. RICKOVER	SSN 795	LAKE ERIE	CG 70
NEW JERSEY	SSN 796	CAPE ST. GEORGE	CG 71
IOWA	SSN 797	VELLA GULF	CG 72
MASSACHUSETTS	SSN 798	PORT ROYAL	CG 73
IDADO	SSN 799		
ARKANSAS	SSN 800	**Destroyers**	
UTAH	SSN 801		
Unnamed	SSN 802	ARLEIGH BURKE	DDG 51
Unnamed	SSN 803	BARRY	DDG 52
Unnamed	SSN 804	JOHN PAUL JONES	DDG 53
Unnamed	SSN 805	CURTIS WILBUR	DDG 54
Unnamed	SSN 806	STOUT	DDG 55
Unnamed	SSN 807	JOHN S. McCAIN	DDG 56
Unnamed	SSN 808	MITSCHER	DDG 57
Unnamed	SSN 809	LABOON	DDG 58

Ship	Hull Number	Ship	Hull Number
RUSSELL	DDG 59	HALSEY	DDG 97
PAUL HAMILTON	DDG 60	FORREST SHERMAN	DDG 98
RAMAGE	DDG 61	FARRAGUT	DDG 99
FITZGERALD	DDG 62	KIDD	DDG 100
STETHEM	DDG 63	GRIDLEY	DDG 101
CARNEY	DDG 64	SAMPSON	DDG 102
BENFOLD	DDG 65	TRUXTUN	DDG 103
GONZALEZ	DDG 66	STERRETT	DDG 104
COLE	DDG 67	DEWEY	DDG 105
THE SULLIVANS	DDG 68	STOCKDALE	DDG 106
MILIUS	DDG 69	GRAVELY	DDG 107
HOPPER	DDG 70	WAYNE E. MEYER	DDG 108
ROSS	DDG 71	JASON DUNHAM	DDG 109
MAHAN	DDG 72	WILLIAM P. LAWRENCE	DDG 110
DECATUR	DDG 73	SPRUANCE	DDG 111
McFAUL	DDG 74	MICHAEL MURPHY	DDG 112
DONALD COOK	DDG 75	JOHN FINN	DDG 113
HIGGINS	DDG 76	RALPH JOHNSON	DDG 114
O'KANE	DDG 77	RAFAEL PERALTA	DDG 115
PORTER	DDG 78	THOMAS HUDNER	DDG 116
OSCAR AUSTIN	DDG 79	PAUL IGNATIUS	DDG 117
ROOSEVELT	DDG 80	DANIEL INOUYE	DDG 118
WINSTON S. CHURCHILL	DDG 81	DELBERT D. BLACK	DDG 119
LASSEN	DDG 82	CARL M. LEVIN	DDG 120
HOWARD	DDG 83	FRANK E. PETERSEN JR	DDG 121
BULKELEY	DDG 84	JOHN BASILONE	DDG 122
McCAMPBELL	DDG 85	LENAH H. SUTCLIFFE HIGBEE	DDG 123
SHOUP	DDG 86		
MASON	DDG 87	HARVEY C. BARNUM JR	DDG 124
PREBLE	DDG 88	JACK H. LUCAS	DDG 125
MUSTIN	DDG 89	LOUISE H. WILSON JR	DDG 126
CHAFEE	DDG 90	PATRICK GALLAGHER	DDG 127
PINCKNEY	DDG 91	TED STEVENS	DDG 128
MOMSEN	DDG 92	JEREMIAH DENTON	DDG 129
CHUNG-HOON	DDG 93	WILLIAM CHARETTE	DDG 130
NITZE	DDG 94	GEORGE M. NEAL	DDG 131
JAMES E. WILLIAMS	DDG 95	QUENTIN WALSH	DDG 132
BAINBRIDGE	DDG 96	SAM NUNN	DDG 133

Ship	Hull Number	Ship	Hull Number
Unnamed	DDG 134	OMAHA	LCS 12
Unnamed	DDG 135	WICHITA	LCS 13
Unnamed	DDG 136	MANCHESTER	LCS 14
Unnamed	DDG 137	BILLINGS	LCS 15
Unnamed	DDG 138	TULSA	LCS 16
		INDIANAPOLIS	LCS 17
ZUMWALT	DDG1000	CHARLESTON	LCS 18
MICHAEL MONSOOR	DDG1001	ST. LOUIS	LCS 19
LYNDON B. JOHNSON	DDG1002	CINCINNATI	LCS 20
		MINNEAPOLIS SAINT-PAUL	LCS 21
Frigates		KANSAS CITY	LCS 22
		COOPERSTOWN	LCS 23
HALYBURTON	FFG 40	OAKLAND	LCS 24
McCLUSKY	FFG 41	MARINETTE	LCS 25
RENTZ	FFG 46	MOBILE	LCS 26
NICHOLAS	FFG 47	NANTUCKET	LCS 27
VANDEGRIFT	FFG 48	SAVANNAH	LCS 28
TAYLOR	FFG 50	BELOIT	LCS 29
GARY	FFG 51	CANBERRA	LCS 30
ELROD	FFG 55	CLEVELAND	LCS 31
SIMPSON	FFG 56	SANTA BARBARA	LCS 32
SAMUEL B. ROBERTS	FFG 58	Unnamed	LCS 33
KAUFFMAN	FFG 59	AUGUSTA	LCS 34
RODNEY M. DAVIS	FFG 60	Unnamed	LCS 35
		KINGSVILLE	LCS 36
Littoral Combat Ships		Unnamed	LCS 37
		PIERRE	LCS 38
FREEDOM	LCS 1		
INDEPENDENCE	LCS 2	**Amphibious Ships**	
FORT WORTH	LCS 3		
CORONADO	LCS 4	BLUE RIDGE	LCC 19
MILWAULKEE	LCS 5	MOUNT WHITNEY	LCC 20
JACKSON	LCS 6		
DETROIT	LCS 7	AMERICA	LHA 6
MONTGOMERY	LCS 8	TRIPOLI	LHA 7
LITTLE ROCK	LCS 9	BOUGAINVILLE	LHA 8
GABRIELLE GIFFORDS	LCS 10		
SIOUX CITY	LCS 11	WASP	LHD 1

Ship	Hull Number	Ship	Hull Number
ESSEX	LHD 2	CHAMPION	MCM 4
KEARSARGE	LHD 3	DEVASTATOR	MCM 6
BOXER	LHD 4	PATRIOT	MCM 7
BATAAN	LHD 5	SCOUT	MCM 8
BONHOMME RICHARD	LHD 6	PIONEER	MCM 9
IWO JIMA	LHD 7	WARRIOR	MCM 10
MAKIN ISLAND	LHD 8	GLADIATOR	MCM 11
		ARDENT	MCM 12
SAN ANTONIO	LPD 17	DEXTROUS	MCM 13
NEW ORLEANS	LPD 18	CHIEF	MCM 14
MESA VERDE	LPD 19		
GREEN BAY	LPD 20	**Patrol Craft**	
NEW YORK	LPD 21		
SAN DIEGO	LPD 22	TEMPEST	PC 2
ANCHORAGE	LPD 23	HURRICANE	PC 3
ARLINGTON	LPD 24	MONSOON	PC 4
SOMERSET	LPD 25	TYPHOON	PC 5
JOHN P. MURTHA	LPD 26	SIROCCO	PC 6
PORTLAND	LPD 27	SQUALL	PC 7
FORT LAUDERDALE	LPD 28	ZEPHYR	PC 8
RICHARD M. McCOOL JR	LPD 29	CHINOOK	PC 9
		FIREBOLT	PC 10
WHIDBEY ISLAND	LSD 41	WHIRLWIND	PC 11
GERMANTOWN	LSD 42	THUNDERBOLT	PC 12
FORT McHENRY	LSD 43	SHAMAL	PC 13
GUNSTON HALL	LSD 44	TORNADO	PC 14
COMSTOCK	LSD 45		
TORTUGA	LSD 46	**Miscellaneous Vessels**	
RUSHMORE	LSD 47		
ASHLAND	LSD 48	SEA FIGHTER	FSF 1
HARPERS FERRY	LSD 49	SEA HUNTER	--
CARTER HALL	LSD 50	SEA HUNTER II	--
OAK HILL	LSD 51	STILLETO	--
PEARL HARBOR	LSD 52	SEA JET	--

Mine Countermeasures Vessels

Submarine Tenders

		EMORY S. LAND	AS 39
SENTRY	MCM 3	FRANK CABLE	AS 40

USS Kentucky

OHIO CLASS SSBN

Ship	Hull Number	Completion Date	Builder
HENRY M. JACKSON	730	1984	GD (Electric Boat Div)
ALABAMA	731	1985	GD (Electric Boat Div)
ALASKA	732	1986	GD (Electric Boat Div)
NEVADA	733	1986	GD (Electric Boat Div)
TENNESSEE	734	1988	GD (Electric Boat Div)
PENNSYLVANIA	735	1989	GD (Electric Boat Div)
WEST VIRGINIA	736	1990	GD (Electric Boat Div)
KENTUCKY	737	1991	GD (Electric Boat Div)
MARYLAND	738	1992	GD (Electric Boat Div)
NEBRASKA	739	1993	GD (Electric Boat Div)
RHODE ISLAND	740	1994	GD (Electric Boat Div)
MAINE	741	1995	GD (Electric Boat Div)
WYOMING	742	1996	GD (Electric Boat Div)
LOUISIANA	743	1997	GD (Electric Boat Div)

Machinery: One nuclear reactor, one shaft **Displacement:** 18,750 tons (dived) **Dimensions:** 170.7m x 12.8m x 11.1m **Speed:** 25+ knots dived **Armament:** 24 - Trident II (D5) missiles, 4 Torpedo Tubes **Complement:** 155

Notes: These fourteen submarines form the US Navy's contribution to the US Nuclear Deterrent Forces. Under normal conditions five of the boats are on patrol at all times, five are in transit for operational areas whilst the remainder are in port undergoing maintenance or refit.

The Trident II/D5 missile is the latest variant of the Trident missile system otherwise known as the Fleet Ballistic Missile, which started as long ago as 1955. The D5 is a three stage missile which is powered by solid rocket propellant. Each inertial guided missile has a range greater than 4,000 miles and has an accuracy measured in hundreds of feet. Trident missiles carry W76 or W88 Multiple Independently Targeted Re-Entry Vehicles (MIRV's). Under the terms of the Strategic Arms Reduction Treaty the US Government has declared that the Trident II/D5 system carries eight MIRV warheads on each missile.

It is planned to start replacing these submarines in the late 2020s with 12 Ohio Replacement or SSBN(X) submarines. These vessels are likely to have the number of launch tubes reduced to 16 but retain the Trident D5 missiles.

Two older Lafayette-class SSBNs, DANIEL WEBSTER and SAM RAYBURN were at Charleston as training vessels for nuclear power systems, though their missile compartments have been removed. They have now been replaced by the Los Angeles-class LA JOLLA and SAN FRANCISCO.

USS Columbia

COLUMBIA CLASS

Ship	Hull Number	Completion Date	Builder
COLUMBIA	SSBN-826	Projected	GD (Electric Boat Div)

Machinery: Nuclear reactor, Turbo electric drive, pump jet **Displacement:** 20,810 tons (submerged) **Dimensions:** 171m x 13.1m x 12m **Speed:** classified **Armament:** 16 launch tubes for Trident D5 missiles; 4 or 6 torpedo tubes **Complement:** 155

Notes: Formerly known as the Ohio Replacement Submarine and the SSBN-X Future Follow on Submarine, the Columbia Class will ultimately replace in front line service the twelve members of the Ohio Class that have been in service since the 1980s. Construction of COLUMBIA, except for long lead items which have already commenced, will start in 2021 with her entry into service scheduled for 2031. Following on from the success of the build sharing arrangement between General Dynamics Electric Boat and Huntington Newport News a similar structure is in place for this submarine building program. In March 2016 General Dynamics was elected as prime contractor for the Columbia Class build and will conduct final assembly of all twelve boats with Huntington Newport News providing between 22 -23 percent of the component parts. Each of the Columbia Class will have sixteen missile tubes for the Trident II D5LE missile. The cost of the program so far has been put at US$4.2 billion, whilst the first of class vessel will cost the American taxpayer in the region of US$6.2 billion. As each subsequent vessel is constructed the US Navy expects this cost to go down to around US$4.9 billion each for the next eleven submarines.

US NAVY/SPECIALIST SEAMAN WILLIAM CARLISLE

USS Michigan

OHIO CLASS SSGN

Ship	Hull Number	Completion Date	Builder
OHIO	726	1981	GD (Electric Boat Div)
MICHIGAN	727	1982	GD (Electric Boat Div)
FLORIDA	728	1983	GD (Electric Boat Div)
GEORGIA	729	1984	GD (Electric Boat Div)

Machinery: One nuclear reactor, one shaft **Displacement:** 18,750 tons (dived) **Dimensions:** 170.7m x 12.8m x 11.1m **Speed:** 20+ knots dived **Armament:** Up to 154 Tomahawk cruise missiles, 4 Torpedo Tubes **Complement:** 169

Notes: In 2003/4 these four former ballistic missile submarines were scheduled for decommissioning, but instead they were converted to serve as land attack submarines with their former Trident missile compartments refitted to serve as launchers for the land attack version of the Tomahawk cruise missile. Up to 154 of these missiles can be stored in each submarine. This class can also support the activities of a team of 66 special forces personnel for up to 90 days and insert and retrieve them clandestinely.

The cost of the conversions was estimated to be approximately US$4 billion for all four vessels.

USS California

ATTACK SUBMARINES
VIRGINIA CLASS

Ship	Hull Number	Completion Date	Builder
BLOCK I			
VIRGINIA	774	2004	GD (Electric Boat Div)
TEXAS	775	2006	Newport News SB
HAWAII	776	2006	GD (Electric Boat Div)
NORTH CAROLINA	777	2007	Newport News SB
BLOCK II			
NEW HAMPSHIRE	778	2008	GD (Electric Boat Div)
NEW MEXICO	779	2010	Newport News SB
MISSOURI	780	2010	GD (Electric Boat Div)
CALIFORNIA	781	2011	Huntington Ingalls
MISSISSIPPI	782	2012	GD (Electric Boat Div)
MINNESOTA	783	2013	Huntington Ingalls
BLOCK III			
NORTH DAKOTA	784	2014	GD (Electric Boat Div)

Ship	Hull Number	Completion Date	Builder
JOHN WARNER	785	2015	Huntington Ingalls
ILLINOIS	786	2016	GD (Electric Boat Div)
WASHINGTON	787	2017	Huntington Ingalls
COLORADO	788	2018	GD (Electric Boat Div)
INDIANA	789	2018	Huntington Ingalls
SOUTH DAKOTA	790	2019	GD (Electric Boat Div)
DELAWARE	791	--	Huntington Ingalls
BLOCK IV			
VERMONT	792	Building	GD (Electric Boat Div)
OREGON	793	Building	GD (Electric Boat Div)
MONTANA	794	Building	Huntington Ingalls
HYMAN G. RICKOVER	795	Building	GD (Electric Boat Div)
NEW JERSEY	796	Building	Huntington Ingalls
IOWA	797	Building	GD (Electric Boat Div)
MASSACHUSETTS	798	Building	GD (Electric Boat Div)
IDAHO	799	Building	GD (Electric Boat Div)
ARKANSAS	800	On order	Huntington Ingalls
UTAH	801	On order	GD (Electric Boat Div)

Machinery: One nuclear reactor, one shaft **Displacement:** 7,800 tons dived **Dimensions:** 114.8m x 10.4m x 8m **Speed:** 25 knots dived **Armament:** Tomahawk missiles, 12 VLS tubes, Mk48 ADCAP torpedoes, 4 Torpedo Tubes **Complement:** 134

Notes: The Virginia Class are progressively replacing the elderly Los Angeles-class submarines in the US fleet. They are large but incredibly stealthy submarines designed to operate in all genres of naval warfare including mining, anti-ship, anti-submarine and intelligence gathering operations. The class have been built in a unique contract sharing arrangement between the two main contractors General Dynamics Electric Boat and Huntington Ingalls Industries Newport News. Under the terms of this teaming arrangement construction is shared for each submarine.

The new nuclear reactor design of the Virginia Class, the S9G Pressurised Water Reactor is expected to run for the entire life of the vessel or around 30 years and will not need an expensive mid-life refuelling.

BLOCK III: BLOCK III saw the introduction of a revised bow shape with the addition of the Large Aperture Bow (LAB) sonar. SOUTH DAKOTA was also the first of the class to be fitted with a propulsor instead of a traditional propeller.

BLOCK IV: The world's most expensive shipbuilding contract was awarded on 28 April 2014 when the US Government ordered 10 Virginia Class Block IV submarines for US$17.6 billion.

BLOCK V: The unnamed SSN802 and SSN 803 were awarded to General Dynamics Electric Boat at Groton in Connecticut on 16 February 2017 whilst a second pair of submarines, the future SSN804 and SSN805 were awarded to Huntington Ingalls Industries at Newport News on 4 May 2017. At the time of writing the first long lead components of the submarines were being manufactured but construction had yet to start on the slipways. A further six Block V vessels (SSN806 - SSN811) are projected but not yet awarded.

BLOCK VI: Block VI will comprise five submarines currently listed as SSN812-SSN816.

BLOCK VII: A further five boats will make up the future Block VII program listed as SSN817- SSN821.

Future designs

Officially the US Navy is targeting a total number of at least thirty Virginia-class attack submarines for the fleet, but it is widely expected to surpass that number in time. Some leading organisations expect that instead of five Block V boats there will instead be double that number built. This could also be the case with Block VI. Some naval commentators expect somewhere in the region of 48 submarines of this class will eventually be built before a successor design is produced towards the end of the current construction program which is set for around 2032.

Other commentators, however, express doubts that the Virginia Class will in fact extend beyond Block V with the so called SSN(X) Improved Virginia Class being ordered into construction instead. This evolved design will draw on the best attributes of the Virginia Class and enhance them with new technologies as they emerge. The first of this class is expected to start construction somewhere in the 2033/34 timeframe and become operational by 2044. One interesting aspect of this new design is the projected use of torpedoes and other extremely long range weapons which will have ranges in excess of 200 nautical miles.

USS Seawolf

SEAWOLF CLASS

Ship	Hull Number	Completion Date	Builder
SEAWOLF	21	1997	GD (Electric Boat Div)
CONNECTICUT	22	1998	GD (Electric Boat Div)
JIMMY CARTER	23	2005	GD (Electric Boat Div)

Machinery: One nuclear reactor, one shaft **Displacement:** 9,284 tons (SSN23: 12,353 tons) **Dimensions:** 108m x 12m x 11m (SSN23 138.07m x 12.2m) **Speed:** 25+ knots
Armament: Tomahawk missiles, Mk48 Torpedoes, 8 torpedo tubes **Complement:** 134

Notes: The Seawolf Class was supposed to be the follow on class from the Los Angeles-class attack submarines and design work on the class was well advanced by the beginning of the 1980s. Their stealth characteristics were designed for the Cold War environment but they came at great cost. When the Cold War ended in 1989 the design was extremely expensive and only three of the class were built with construction of SEAWOLF starting in 1989. JIMMY CARTER is longer and heavier than the other two vessels due to the insertion of a special forces block that incorporates advanced technologies and allows the submarine to insert and retrieve special forces clandestinely. Fifty special forces personnel can be accommodated on board SSN23 alongside their special vehicles. SSN23 also features special intelligence gathering equipment.

USS Topeka

LOS ANGELES CLASS

Ship	Hull Number	Completion Date	Builder
BREMERTON	698	1981	GD (Electric Boat Div)
OLYMPIA	717	1984	Newport News SB
PROVIDENCE	719	1985	GD (Electric Boat Div)
CHICAGO	721	1986	Newport News SB
KEY WEST	722	1987	Newport News SB
OKLAHOMA CITY	723	1988	Newport News SB
LOUISVILLE	724	1986	GD (Electric Boat Div)
HELENA	725	1987	GD (Electric Boat Div)
NEWPORT NEWS	750	1989	Newport News SB
SAN JUAN	751	1988	GD (Electric Boat Div)
PASADENA	752	1989	GD (Electric Boat Div)
ALBANY	753	1990	Newport News SB
TOPEKA	754	1989	GD (Electric Boat Div)
SCRANTON	756	1991	Newport News SB
ALEXANDRIA	757	1991	GD (Electric Boat Div)

Ship	Hull Number	Completion Date	Builder
ASHEVILLE	758	1991	Newport News SB
JEFFERSON CITY	759	1992	Newport News SB
ANNAPOLIS	760	1992	GD (Electric Boat Div)
SPRINGFIELD	761	1993	GD (Electric Boat Div)
COLUMBUS	762	1993	GD (Electric Boat Div)
SANTA FE	763	1994	GD (Electric Boat Div)
BOISE	764	1992	Newport News SB
MONTPELIER	765	1993	Newport News SB
CHARLOTTE	766	1994	Newport News SB
HAMPTON	767	1993	Newport News SB
HARTFORD	768	1994	GD (Electric Boat Div)
TOLEDO	769	1995	Newport News SB
TUCSON	770	1995	Newport News SB
COLUMBIA	771	1995	GD (Electric Boat Div)
GREENVILLE	772	1996	Newport News SB
CHEYENNE	773	1996	Newport News SB

Machinery: One nuclear reactor, one shaft **Displacement:** 7,011 tonnes **Dimensions:** 110m x 10m x 9.7m **Speed:** 20+ knots **Armament:** Tomahawk missiles, vertical launch tubes (719 and later) Mk 48 torpedoes, four torpedo tubes **Complement:** 140

Notes: This class was designed in the 1960s as a replacement for the Sturgeon Class and featured vastly improved sound quietening technology over previous classes. Her larger propulsion plant gave improved speed and endurance and allowed for a greater number of electrically hungry components to be included in the design. As the design evolved the Los Angeles Class became masters of every genre of naval warfare from anti submarine, anti surface ship, mining operations, special forces delivery as well as intelligence gathering.

As with any design of submarine that has a build stretching over three decades, the design evolved over time, eventually three distinct variants emerged. From PROVIDENCE onwards the submarines were equipped with a dozen vertical launch tubes for the Tomahawk land attack missile as well as an upgraded core for their nuclear reactors. The final 23 hulls comprise the Improved Los Angeles Class or 688I Class. These boats have the superlative BSY-1 bow mounted sonar and the ability to lay minefields with their torpedo tubes. Another unique design feature is that the diving planes previously positioned on the submarine's sail were placed on the bow, whilst the sail itself was strengthened to allow it to penetrate through thick pack ice for Arctic operations.

BREMERTON and PROVIDENCE are scheduled to decommission in 2019. Former sister ships LA JOLLA completed a conversion in 2018 to become an alongside training ship whilst SAN FRANCISCO commenced a similar conversion in 2018.

Notes on Decommissioning
By law US nuclear-powered vessels must have crews onboard until their reactors have been defuelled. Therefore, when USN submarines are withdrawn from service they are placed "In Commission, In Reserve." Once defuelled and de-equipped they can be decommissioned and removed (stricken) from the Navy Register. Vessels "In Commission, In Reserve" cannot be recalled to active duty.

Submarine Rescue
Based at San Diego, and operated by the Navy's Deep Submergence Unit, The Submarine Rescue Diving and Recompression Systems (SRDRS) is a rapidly deployable rescue asset that can be delivered by air or ground, installed on pre-screened military or commercial vessels of opportunity (VOO) via a ship interface template, and mated to a distressed submarine within a 72-hour time to first rescue period.

It comprises the Atmospheric Dive System 2000 (ADS2000) which was delivered to the Navy in 2006. ADS2000 is a manned, one-atmosphere dive suit capable of inspecting disabled submarines and clearing debris from escape hatches. The RCS (Rescue Capable System) constitutes the SRDRS second phase. SRDRS-RCS consists of FALCON, a tethered, remotely-operated Pressurised Rescue Module (PRM), its launch and recovery system, and its support equipment; all of which are controlled from a VOO.

The final phase of the SRDRS program is the Submarine Decompression System (SDS). This allows rescued submariners to remain under pressure during the transfer from the PRM to hyperbaric treatment chambers aboard the VOO.

SRDRS is a "fly-away" system that can quickly and easily be mobilised via large military or civilian transport aircraft and installed aboard a variety of VOOs within hours of notification of a submarine in distress.

FALCON can conduct rescue operations to a depth of 2,000 feet, can mate to a disabled submarine at a list and trim of up to 45 degrees, and can transfer up to 16 personnel at a time. Because SRDRS-RCS receives its power from a VOO via an umbilical, it can operate around the clock without pause.

USS Gerald R. Ford

AIRCRAFT CARRIERS
GERALD R. FORD CLASS

Ship	Hull Number	Completion Date	Builder
GERALD R. FORD	CVN 78	2015	Huntington Ingalls
JOHN F. KENNEDY	CVN 79	2023	Huntington Ingalls
ENTERPRISE	CVN 80	2025	Huntington Ingalls
UNNAMED	CVN 81	On order	Huntington Ingalls
UNNAMED	CVN 82	On order	Huntington Ingalls

Machinery: Two Bechtel A1B nuclear reactors driving four shafts **Displacement:** 100,000 tons full load **Dimensions:** 337m x 41m (Flight Deck width 78m) x 12m **Speed:** 30+ knots **Armament:** Two RIM0162 ESSM launchers, 2 x RIM-116 RAM launchers, 3 Phalanx 20 mm CIWS mounts, 4 Mk2 50cal machine guns **Aircraft:** 75+ **Complement:** 508 officers, 3,789 enlisted

Notes: The Gerald R. Ford-class aircraft carriers are the first new aircraft carrier in the US Navy for five decades. The ship also introduced a wide number of innovations over the previous Nimitz-class ships and as such will not be fully operational for a number of years until she completes first of class trials.

Notable design changes over the Nimitz Class include the re-positioning of the island further aft to improve the efficiency of flight deck operations as well as the use, for the first time anywhere, of EMALS (Electromagnetic Aircraft Launch System), which does away with the expensive and high maintenance steam catapults of earlier aircraft carriers. GERALD R. FORD also has advanced landing gear systems and AN/SPY-3 X Band multi function radar. Less visible changes to the ship have included greater use of automation which has had a consequent reduction in crew complement.

The new Bechtel A1B nuclear reactors, two of which are included in each of the ships of the class have a design life that of the ship itself which is projected to be in service for around 50 years. Furthermore the new reactor type provides 25 percent greater electrical output than the earlier designs on board Nimitz-class ships.

USS Carl Vinson

AIRCRAFT CARRIERS
NIMITZ CLASS

Ship	Hull Number	Completion Date	Builder
NIMITZ	CVN 68	1975	Newport News SB
DWIGHT D. EISENHOWER	CVN 69	1977	Newport News SB
CARL VINSON	CVN 70	1982	Newport News SB
THEODORE ROOSEVELT	CVN 71	1986	Newport News SB
ABRAHAM LINCOLN	CVN 72	1989	Newport News SB
GEORGE WASHINGTON	CVN 73	1992	Newport News SB
JOHN C. STENNIS	CVN 74	1995	Newport News SB
HARRY S. TRUMAN	CVN 75	1998	Newport News SB
RONALD REAGAN	CVN 76	2003	Newport News SB
GEORGE H.W. BUSH	CVN 77	2008	Newport News SB

Machinery: Two nuclear reactors driving four shafts   **Displacement:** 91,487 tons full load (CVN 68-70), 96,386 tons full load (CVN 71), 102,000 tons full load (CVN 72-74) **Dimensions:** 332.9m x 40.8m x 11.3m (CVN 68-70) 11.8m (CVN 71) 11.9m (CVN 72-74) **Speed:** 30+ knots **Armament:** Two or three (depending on modifications) NATO Sea Sparrow launchers, 20mm Phalanx CIWS mounts: (3 on CVN 68 and CVN 69, 4 on later ships.) **Aircraft:** 85 **Complement:** 3,200 plus 2,480 air wing.

Notes: First designs emerged for this class in the early 1960s following the completion of the world's first nuclear powered aircraft carrier USS ENTERPRISE. NIMITZ is now nearing the end of her service life and is expected to be replaced by the new USS ENTERPRISE in service sometime in 2022.

This class is expected to operate for around 15 years between refuellings. Over the five decades since the first of the class entered service significant modifications to the design have been made including the addition of a prominent bow bulb on RONALD REAGAN and GEORGE H. W. BUSH designed to improve general seakeeping. On these vessels the island structure has also been redesigned which has resulted in it being one deck lower than on previous ships of the class. All ships of the Nimitz Class have four powerful steam catapults, two forward and two in the waist of the ship. RONALD REAGAN and GEORGE H. W. BUSH have also been equipped with larger 'one piece' jet deflectors. A revised deck layout has also been introduced on these ships that has shifted the orientation further towards the port side of the ships. This was facilitated by the addition of a longer angled deck extension which permitted simultaneous landing and take off operations.

In the past, Nimitz-class aircraft carriers were at the centre of a Carrier Battle Group which comprised layers of cruisers, destroyers, frigates, support vessels and submarines. Today a somewhat streamlined Carrier Strike Group (CSG) offers a more flexible approach.

USS San Jacinto

CRUISERS
TICONDEROGA CLASS

Ship	Hull Number	Completion Date	Builder
BUNKER HILL	CG 52	1986	Ingalls SB
MOBILE BAY	CG 53	1987	Ingalls SB
ANTIETAM	CG 54	1987	Ingalls SB
LEYTE GULF	CG 55	1987	Ingalls SB
SAN JACINTO	CG 56	1988	Ingalls SB
LAKE CHAMPLAIN	CG 57	1988	Ingalls SB
PHILIPPINE SEA	CG 58	1989	Bath Iron Works
PRINCETON	CG 59	1989	Ingalls SB
NORMANDY	CG 60	1989	Bath Iron Works
MONTEREY	CG 61 ·	1990	Bath Iron Works
CHANCELLORSVILLE	CG 62	1989	Ingalls SB
COWPENS	CG 63	1991	Bath Iron Works
GETTYSBURG	CG 64	1991	Bath Iron Works

Ship	Hull Number	Completion Date	Builder
CHOSIN	CG 65	1991	Ingalls SB
HUE CITY	CG 66	1991	Ingalls SB
SHILOH	CG 67 •	1992	Bath Iron Works
ANZIO	CG 68	1992	Ingalls SB
VICKSBURG	CG 69	1992	Ingalls SB
LAKE ERIE	CG 70 •	1993	Bath Iron Works
CAPE ST. GEORGE	CG 71	1993	Ingalls SB
VELLA GULF	CG 72 •	1993	Ingalls SB
PORT ROYAL	CG 73 •	1994	Ingalls SB

Machinery: Four General Electric LM2500 gas turbine engines; two shafts, 80,000 shp **Displacement:** 9,600 tons **Dimensions:** 172.8m x 16.8m x 9.5m **Speed:** 30+ knots **Armament:** Mk 41 VLS Standard Missile (MR); Vertical Launch ASROC missiles; Tomahawk Cruise missiles; Six Mk46 torpedoes (two triple mounts); Two Mk 45 5-inch/62 calibre guns; Two Phalanx CIWS **Aircraft:** Two SH-60/MH-60 Seahawk **Complement:** 364

Notes: The Ticonderoga-class cruisers are the multi-purpose vessels of the fleet designed to operate as part of a battle group. These ships can perform anti-air, anti-submarine, anti-surface and long strike roles whilst usually as part of a battle strike group, although they can also operate independently. In the last few years the ships have been subject to hull, mechanical and electrical system upgrades and at least eight have also had combat system upgrades including Aegis system with the SPQ-9B radar system. Additionally a number have had modifications made to their vertical launch systems to allow them to fire the RIM-162 ESSM missile as well as the fitting of the SQQ-89A (V)15 sonar and multi function towed array sonar. These upgrades cost US$250 million per ship.

These somewhat elderly vessels are increasingly hard to maintain but there is no current replacement program in place and through life extension programs the US Navy expects to keep the Ticonderoga cruisers operational through to 2035-45 time frame. In late 2018 the US Navy's Chief of Naval Operations Director of Surface Warfare (OPNAV N96) convened a large surface combatant requirements evaluation team to assess the requirements for a future cruiser to replace the Ticonderoga Class with the intention to replace the first of these venerable vessels in 2023 or 2024. It appears that some things are certain about the replacement designs. The US Navy is looking to the future and wants a vessel that can be easily and relatively cheaply upgraded. The new ships will be power hungry as they are likely to be equipped with energy intensive weapons such as electromagnetic rail guns and laser weapons. They are also likely to be larger than the existing ships as this option allows for greater flexibility and future growth. Any new vessel would most likely take the best aspects of both the Arleigh Burke-class destroyers and the Zumwalt-class destroyers.

USS Michael Monsoor

DESTROYERS
ZUMWALT CLASS

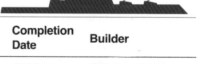

Ship	Hull Number	Completion Date	Builder
ZUMWALT	DDG 1000	*2016*	Bath Iron Works
MICHAEL MONSOOR	DDG 1001	*2019*	Bath Iron Works
LYNDON B. JOHNSON	DDG 1002	Building	Bath Iron Works

Machinery: 2 Rolls Royce MT30 gas turbines driving Curtiss Wright electric generators; 2 Rolls Royce RR4500 turbine generators, 2 shafts **Displacement:** 15,995 tons full load **Dimensions:** 190m x 24m x 8.4m **Speed:** 30+ knots **Armament:** 20 Mk57 VLS Modules for a total of 80 launch cells; RIM-162 Evolved Sea Sparrow; Tactical Tomahawk missiles; Vertical launch anti submarine Missile (ASROC); 2x 155mm (6inch)/62 calibre Advanced Gun System with 920 round magazine **Aircraft:** 1 x SH-60 helicopter; 3 x MQ-8 Fire Scout VT UAV **Complement:** 147 + 28 air detachment

Notes: This class of large guided missile cruiser was designed to provide the US Navy with an overpowering land attack capability together with unrivalled levels of stealth. Originally projected to be a class of 32 such ships, the program was then cut back to 24, then 7 and eventually to just three as costs escalated during the design and development phase of the program. In April 2016, the U.S. Naval Institute stated the total cost of the three Zumwalt ships is about US$22.5 billion with research and development costs, which is an average of US$7.5 billion per ship. Each of the three completed ships were designed around the two Advanced Gun Systems and their unique Long Range Land Attack Projectile (LRLAP) ammunition. Unfortunately, the LRLAP procurement was subsequently cancelled leading to the US Navy to repurpose these weapons for the surface warfare role.

The Zumwalt Class has a distinctive appearance with a wave piercing tumblehome hull form and inward sloping hull sides to provide an exceptionally low radar cross section. Each of the ships is powered by an integrated power system which can send electricity to any part of the ship that requires it. This has led to a large decrease in the ship's complement.

US NAVY / MSC2 CHARLES OKI

USS Zumwalt

USS Porter

ARLEIGH BURKE CLASS
Flight I & Flight II

Ship	Hull Number	Completion Date	Builder
ARLEIGH BURKE	DDG 51	1991	Bath Iron Works
BARRY	DDG 52	1992	Ingalls SB
JOHN PAUL JONES	DDG 53 ·	1993	Bath Iron Works
CURTIS WILBUR	DDG 54 ·	1994	Bath Iron Works
STOUT	DDG 55 ·	1994	Ingalls SB
JOHN S. McCAIN	DDG 56 ·	1994	Bath Iron Works
MITSCHER	DDG 57	1995	Ingalls SB
LABOON	DDG 58	1995	Bath Iron Works
RUSSELL	DDG 59 ·	1995	Ingalls SB
PAUL HAMILTON	DDG 60 ·	1995	Bath Iron Works
RAMAGE	DDG 61 ·	1995	Ingalls SB
FITZGERALD	DDG 62 ·	1995	Bath Iron Works
STETHEM	DDG 63 ·	1995	Ingalls SB
CARNEY	DDG 64 ·	1996	Bath Iron Works
BENFOLD	DDG 65 ·	1996	Ingalls SB

Ship	Hull Number	Completion Date	Builder
GONZALEZ	DDG 66	1996	Bath Iron Works
COLE	DDG 67 •	1996	Ingalls SB
THE SULLIVANS	DDG 68	1997	Bath Iron Works
MILIUS	DDG 69 •	1996	Ingalls SB
HOPPER	DDG 70 •	1997	Bath Iron Works
ROSS	DDG 71 •	1997	Ingalls SB
MAHAN	DDG 72	1998	Bath Iron Works
DECATUR	DDG 73 •	1998	Bath Iron Works
McFAUL	DDG 74 •	1998	Ingalls SB
DONALD COOK	DDG 75 •	1998	Bath Iron Works
HIGGINS	DDG 76 •	1999	Bath Iron Works
O'KANE	DDG 77 •	1999	Bath Iron Works
PORTER	DDG 78 •	1999	Ingalls SB

• Indicates BMD capable vessels

Machinery: Four GE LM2500-30 gas turbines; two shafts; 100,000 shp **Displacement:** 9,033 tons **Dimensions:** 153.92m x 18m x 6.3m **Speed:** 30+ knots **Armament:** Mk 41 VLS Standard missile; Harpoon; VLS ASROC missiles; Tomahawk; six Mk 46 torpedoes (two triple tube mounts); one 5-inch/54 calibre gun **Aircraft:** Landing facilities aft, but no hangar **Complement:** 323

Notes: The Arleigh Burke-class destroyers have become the most numerous class of ship within the US Navy and as a consequence have been utilised the most around the globe. These vessels are heavily armed and are multi-purpose ships that can operate as part of a task group or independently and in all warfare fighting roles. The design of the ships was centred around the use of the SPY-1D, multi-function phased array radar system and linked to the Aegis combat system deep within the ships. From MAHAN (Flight II ships) onwards the ships were further enhanced with the installation of Link 16, SLQ-32(V) electronic warfare suite, extended range missiles and better inter ship and other friendly forces communications. The Flight II ships also benefit from having extra reserves of fuel over the Flight I ships thus greatly extending their range.

The USN has refitted a number of these ships to serve as firing ships as part of the Anti Ballistic Missile program. The ships concerned have seen an enhanced Aegis system and the SM-3 missile, enabling the ships to serve as the launching point for missiles targeting ballistic missiles in space.

USS Winston S. Churchill

ARLEIGH BURKE CLASS
Flight IIA

Ship	Hull Number	Completion Date	Builder
OSCAR AUSTIN	DDG 79	2000	Bath Iron Works
ROOSEVELT	DDG 80	2000	Ingalls SB
WINSTON S. CHURCHILL	DDG 81	2001	Bath Iron Works
LASSEN	DDG 82	2001	Ingalls SB
HOWARD	DDG 83	2001	Bath Iron Works
BULKELEY	DDG 84	2001	Ingalls SB
McCAMPBELL	DDG 85	2002	Bath Iron Works
SHOUP	DDG 86	2002	Ingalls SB
MASON	DDG 87	2003	Bath Iron Works
PREBLE	DDG 88	2002	Ingalls SB
MUSTIN	DDG 89	2003	Ingalls SB
CHAFEE	DDG 90	2003	Bath Iron Works
PINCKNEY	DDG 91	2004	Ingalls SB

Ship	Hull Number	Completion Date	Builder
MOMSEN	DDG 92	2004	Bath Iron Works
CHUNG-HOON	DDG 93	2004	Ingalls SB
NITZE	DDG 94	2004	Bath Iron Works
JAMES E. WILLIAMS	DDG 95	2004	Ingalls SB
BAINBRIDGE	DDG 96	2005	Bath Iron Works
HALSEY	DDG 97	2005	Ingalls SB
FORREST SHERMAN	DDG 98	2006	Ingalls SB
FARRAGUT	DDG 99	2006	Bath Iron Works
KIDD	DDG 100	2006	Ingalls SB
GRIDLEY	DDG 101	2006	Bath Iron Works
SAMPSON	DDG 102	2007	Bath Iron Works
TRUXTUN	DDG 103	2007	Ingalls SB
STERETT	DDG 104	2007	Bath Iron Works
DEWEY	DDG 105	2008	Ingalls SB
STOCKDALE	DDG 106	2008	Bath Iron Works
GRAVELY	DDG 107	2009	Ingalls SB
WAYNE E. MEYER	DDG 108	2009	Bath Iron Works
JASON DUNHAM	DDG 109	2010	Bath Iron Works
WILLIAM P. LAWRENCE	DDG 110	2011	Ingalls SB
SPRUANCE	DDG 111	2011	Bath Iron Works
MICHAEL MURPHY	DDG 112	2012	Bath Iron Works
JOHN FINN	DDG 113	2017	Ingalls SB
RALPH JOHNSON	DDG 114	2018	Ingalls SB
RAFAEL PERALTA	DDG 115	2017	Bath Iron Works
THOMAS HUDNER	DDG 116	2018	Bath Iron Works
PAUL IGNATIUS	DDG 117	2018	Ingalls SB
DANIEL INOUYE	DDG 118	2020	Bath Iron Works
DELBERT D. BLACK	DDG 119	Building	Ingalls SB
CARL M. LEVIN	DDG 120	Building	Bath Iron Works
FRANK E. PETERSEN JR	DDG 121	Building	Ingalls SB

Ship	Hull Number	Completion Date	Builder
JOHN BASILONE	DDG 122	Building	Bath Iron Works
LENAH H. SUTCLIFFE-HIGBEE	DDG 123	Building	Ingalls SB
HARVEY C. BARNUM JR	DDG 124	Building	Bath Iron Works

Machinery: Four GE LM 2500-30 gas turbines; Two shafts; 100,000 shp **Displacement:** 9,217 tons **Dimensions:** 155.3m x 20.4m x 6.3m **Speed:** 30+ knots **Armament:** Mk 41 VLS Standard missile; Harpoon; VLS ASROC missiles; Tomahawk; six Mk 46 torpedoes (two triple tube mounts); one 5-inch/54 calibre gun **Aircraft:** Two SH-60 Seahawk helicopters **Complement:** 323

Notes: This class of destroyers are similar to the previous Flight Is. In 2016 the US Navy announced that these ships would be refitted with a hybrid electric drive (HED) which would reduce fuel costs. The four LM-2500 gas turbines will be retained but augmented with an electric motor attached to the main reduction gear to turn the ship's main drive shafts at speeds lower than 13 knots. The knock on benefits mean that the ships can loiter on station for up to 2.5 more days than previously before requiring refuelling. USS TRUXTON (DDG-103) was the first of this Flight to receive the package. Sadly, in March 2018, the program was halted leaving TRUXTON as a test demonstrator for the new technologies.

In 2016 PORTER, CARNEY, ROSS and DONALD COOK received significant self-protection upgrades and saw their legacy Phalanx CIWS replaced with the SeaRam close range missile system. Lockheed Martin, in February 2018, were contracted to deliver their High Energy Laser and Integrated Optical dazzler with Surveillance (HELIOS) system. The laser can generate 60-150 kW of power to dazzle or destroy small boats and Unmanned Aerial Vehicles. It is expected that the first HELIOS system will be delivered in 2020.

USS Arleigh Burke

ARLEIGH BURKE CLASS
Flight III & Flight IIA TI

Ship	Hull Number	Completion Date	Builder
JACK H. LUCAS	DDG 125	Contracted	Ingalls SB
LOUISE H. WILSON JR	DDG 126	Contracted	Bath Iron Works
PATRICK GALLAGHER	DDG 127	Ordered	Bath Iron Works
TED STEVENS	DDG 128	Ordered	Ingalls SB
JEREMIAH DENTON	DDG 129	Ordered	Ingalls SB
WILLIAM CHARETTE	DDG 130	Ordered	Bath Iron Works
GEORGE M. NEAL	DDG 131	Ordered	Ingalls SB
QUENTIN WALSH	DDG 132	Ordered	Bath Iron Works
SAM NUNN	DDG 133	Ordered	Ingalls SB

Machinery: Two GE LM2500-30 gas turbine engines; 2 shafts; 41,000 shp
Displacement: 9,217 tonnes **Dimensions:** 155.3m x 20.4m x 6.3m **Speed:** 30+ knots
Armament: Mk 41 VLS Standard missile; Harpoon; VLS ASROC missiles; Tomahawk;
six Mk46 torpedoes (two triple tube mounts); one 5-inch/54 calibre gun **Aircraft:** Two
SH-60 Seahawk helicopters **Complement:** 323

USS Billings

LITTORAL COMBAT SHIPS
FREEDOM CLASS

Ship	Hull Number	Completion Date	Builder
FREEDOM	LCS 1	2008	LM/Marinette Marine Shipyard
FORT WORTH	LCS 3	2012	LM/Marinette Marine Shipyard
MILWAULKEE	LCS 5	2015	LM/Marinette Marine Shipyard
DETROIT	LCS 7	2015	LM/Marinette Marine Shipyard
LITTLE ROCK	LCS 9	2016	LM/Marinette Marine Shipyard
SIOUX CITY	LCS 11	2017	LM/Marinette Marine Shipyard
WICHITA	LCS 13	Building	LM/Marinette Marine Shipyard
BILLINGS	LCS 15	Building	LM/Marinette Marine Shipyard
INDIANAPOLIS	LCS 17	Building	LM/Marinette Marine Shipyard
ST. LOUIS	LCS 19	Building	LM/Marinette Marine Shipyard
MINNEAPOLIS-ST PAUL	LCS 21	Building	LM/Marinette Marine Shipyard
COOPERSTOWN	LCS 23	Building	LM/Marinette Marine Shipyard
MARINETTE	LCS 25	Building	LM/Marinette Marine Shipyard
NANTUCKET	LCS 27	Building	LM/Marinette Marine Shipyard

Ship	Hull Number	Completion Date	Builder
BELOIT	LCS 29	Building	LM/Marinette Marine Shipyard
CLEVELAND	LCS 31	Building	LM/Marinette Marine Shipyard

Machinery: Combined diesel and gas turbine with steerable water jet propulsion **Displacement:** 3,000 tonnes **Dimensions:** 115m x 13m x 4m **Speed:** 45+ knots **Armament:** One Bofors 57mm; One RAM launcher; Four .50 calibre Mg; additional weapons can be added depending on role **Complement:** 15 core crew (up to 75 max.)

Notes: In 2006 the US Navy awarded two contracts for two separate designs for Littoral Combat ships with the aim to replace the Oliver Hazard Perry-class frigates in service. The original aim was to construct up to 60 vessels. The Freedom Class was designed by Lockheed Martin and is for a semi planing steel mono hull. The vessel's weapons and sensors can be reconfigured due to its modular design dependent upon the tasking required of the ship and can be completed in short order (up to 24 hours in some cases). The Freedom Class can be fitted to serve in anti-submarine, anti-surface, mine warfare or surveillance roles.

All the ships of this class will bear the names of small and medium sized US cities.

In 2015 a redesigned version of the Freedom Class successfully was sold to Saudi Arabia who placed an order for four of the vessels.

In October 2018 the US Navy announced that the name USS CLEVELAND had been allocated to the Littoral Combat ship program but did not specify whether the ship would be a Freedom or an Independence-class vessel.

The first ships were delivered before the designs were mature, so some modifications and design changes have been incorporated into later vessels following experience with FREEDOM (LCS 1). Starting with FORT WORTH (LCS 3), the transom was lengthened and buoyancy tanks added to the stern to enhance stability. From MILWAUKEE (LCS 5) onward the class is to be fitted with cavitation performance waterjets and a less complex gas turbine electric start system to reduce costs and lower ship weight.

There is still much debate centred around the survivability of these ships and the practicality of relying on palletised mission equipment. As of 2014 it would appear that the US Navy is looking at a more robust and capable vessel to replace the FFG 7 class frigate and the predicted total buy of LCS has now been reduced from 50 to 32 ships.

USS Manchester

LITTORAL COMBAT SHIPS
INDEPENDENCE CLASS

Ship	Hull Number	Completion Date	Builder
INDEPENDENCE	LCS 2	2010	GD/ Austal USA
CORONADO	LCS 4	2014	GD/ Austal USA
JACKSON	LCS 6	2015	GD/ Austal USA
MONTGOMERY	LCS 8	2016	GD/ Austal USA
GABRIELLE GIFFORDS	LCS 10	2017	GD/ Austal USA
OMAHA	LCS 12	2018	GD/ Austal USA
MANCHESTER	LCS 14	2018	GD/ Austal USA
TULSA	LCS 16	Building	GD/ Austal USA
CHARLESTON	LCS 18	Building	GD/ Austal USA
CINCINNATI	LCS 20	Building	GD/ Austal USA
KANSAS CITY	LCS 22	Building	GD/ Austal USA
OAKLAND	LCS 24	Building	GD/ Austal USA
MOBILE	LCS 26	Building	GD/ Austal USA
SAVANNAH	LCS 28	Building	GD/ Austal USA

Ship	Hull Number	Completion Date	Builder
CANBERRA	LCS 30	Building	GD/ Austal USA
SANTA BARBARA	LCS 32	Building	GD/ Austal USA

Machinery: Combined diesel and Gas Turbines with steerable waterjet propulsion **Displacement:** 2,800 tonnes **Dimensions:** 127.1m x 30.4m x 4.5m **Speed:** 45 knots **Armament:** One Bofors 57mm; One RAM launcher; Four .50 calibre MG; additional weapons can be added depending on role **Aircraft:** 2 x MH-60R/S Seahawk or CH-53 Sea Stallion **Complement:** 50 core crew (up to 75)

Notes: The second of two designs for the Littoral Combat Ship role within the US Navy. This design built by General Dynamics and Austal USA features a trimaran hull form made out of aluminium. A large flight deck on the stern allows these ships to operate large helicopters to up to the size of the CH-53 Sea Stallion.

In May 2018 it was announced that from 2019 this class of ships would in future be referred to as Fast Frigates (FF).

The aluminium trimaran design offers a large flight deck and helicopter handling capability on a relatively small displacement vessel, the hangar being able to accommodate two Seahawk helicopters, while the flight deck can handle larger helicopters.

The unique trimaran design has many advantages over a single hull, the main one being the interior volume available. The mission bay is 1,410 m^2, and takes up most of the deck below the hangar and flight deck. With 11,000 cubic metres of payload volume, it is able to carry out one mission, while storing a separate mission module, allowing the ship to conduct multiple missions without having to be refitted. Accommodation spaces are located below the bridge structure. One of the drawbacks of the design is the narrow bridge and the lack of bridge wings, something that will be rectified in future ships of the class.

Like the Freedom Class, these ships will be getting axial flow water jets, which push water parallel to the shaft of the impeller, to improve efficiency and reduce maintenance. After the lead ship of the class suffered from aggressive disintegration due to galvanic corrosion, Austal has made changes to the remaining ships in the class. CORONADO (LCS 4) received new anti-corrosion surface treatments, while JACKSON (LCS 6) will have an array of tested corrosion-management tools and processes.

USS Patriot

MINE COUNTERMEASURES SHIPS
AVENGER CLASS

Ship	Hull Number	Completion Date	Builder
SENTRY	MCM 3	1989	Peterson Builders Inc.
CHAMPION	MCM 4	1991	Marinette Marine Corp.
DEVASTATOR	MCM 6	1990	Peterson Builders Inc.
PATRIOT	MCM 7	1991	Marinette Marine Corp.
SCOUT	MCM 8	1990	Peterson Builders Inc.
PIONEER	MCM 9	1992	Peterson Builders Inc.
WARRIOR	MCM 10	1993	Peterson Builders Inc.
GLADIATOR	MCM 11	1993	Peterson Builders Inc
ARDENT	MCM 12	1994	Peterson Builders Inc.
DEXTROUS	MCM 13	1994	Peterson Builders Inc.
CHIEF	MCM 14	1994	Peterson Builders Inc.

Machinery: Four diesels (each 600shp); Twin shaft with controllable pitch propellers
Displacement: 1,450 tons **Dimensions:** 68.4m x 11.9m x 3.7m **Speed:** 13.5 knots

Armament: 2 x 12.7 MG (MCM11 1 x 25mm 88 Bushmaster; 1 x 7.63 Gatling MG)
Complement: 84

Notes: Designed as minehunter-killers capable of finding, classifying and destroying moored and bottom mines. They retain a conventional minesweeping capability.

The hulls of the ships are constructed of oak, Douglas fir and Nookta Cypress wood with a thin coating of fibreglass in order to reduce the magnetic signature of these vessels.

Since 2004 the class has been progressively upgraded and has seen their original engines replaced with more powerful and environmentally friendly modern units.

CHIEF, PATRIOT, PIONEER and WARRIOR are forward deployed to Sasebo, Japan while DEVASTATOR, DEXTROUS, GLADIATOR and SENTRY are forward deployed to Manama, Bahrain. ARDENT, SCOUT and CHAMPION are located at their home port of San Diego, California. CHAMPION is scheduled to be decommissioned in 2019.

USS Zephyr

PATROL SHIPS (COASTAL)
CYCLONE CLASS

Ship	Hull Number	Completion Date	Builder
TEMPEST	PC 2	1993	Bollinger, Lockport
HURRICANE	PC 3	1993	Bollinger, Lockport
MONSOON	PC 4	1993	Bollinger, Lockport
TYPHOON	PC 5	1994	Bollinger, Lockport
SIROCCO	PC 6	1994	Bollinger, Lockport
SQUALL	PC 7	1994	Bollinger, Lockport
ZEPHYR	PC 8	1994	Bollinger, Lockport
CHINOOK	PC 9	1995	Bollinger, Lockport
FIREBOLT	PC 10	1995	Bollinger, Lockport
WHIRLWIND	PC 11	1995	Bollinger, Lockport
THUNDERBOLT	PC 12	1995	Bollinger, Lockport
SHAMAL	PC 13	1996	Bollinger, Lockport
TORNADO	PC 14	2000	Bollinger, Lockport

Machinery: Four Paxman diesels; four shafts; 3,350 shp **Displacement:** 336 tonnes **Dimensions:** 51.8m x 7.6m x 2.4m **Speed:** 35 knots **Armament:** One Mk 96 and one Mk 28 25mm MG; Five .50 cal MG; two Mk 19 40mm automatic grenade launcher; two M-60 machine guns; 6 FIM 92 Stinger Surface to air missiles; 2 Mk60 quadruple BGM-176BB Griffin B surface to surface missile launchers **Complement:** 28

Notes: In the last decade with the US Navy's change of focus from blue water operations to one directed towards the littoral regions, this class has come into its own. For a while in the 1990s, however, this class was looking out of place in a fleet dominated by deep water deployments. Today with coastal patrol and interdiction and surveillance a priority in the fight against international terrorism, drug and people smuggling, this class looks like it has a healthy future.

Originally to have comprised 16 vessels, two were subsequently cancelled and the lead ship of the class CYCLONE was sold in 2003 to the Philippine Navy taking the name of BRP MARINA ALVAREZ.

Most of the class are forward deployed to the Persian Gulf with three ships TORNADO, SHAMAL and ZEPHYR based at Mayport in Florida.

COASTAL RIVERINE FORCE

During the Vietnam War of the 1960s and 1970s the US Navy and US Marine Corps developed a force of small, highly mobile and agile riverine forces. Sadly, over time that force was allowed to whittle away to nothing, but in the early 2000s it was re-established as a means to combat unconventional warfare such as terrorist attacks and for operations in the Middle East and elsewhere.

The Riverine Squadrons were re-established in 2006 as an element of the US Navy's Expeditionary Combat Command (NECC). Their role is to conduct Theatre Security Cooperation and Maritime Security Operations. Six years later the Coastal Riverine Force (CRF) was created following the merging of the existing Maritime Expeditionary Security Force and the Navy Riverine Force.

CRF is based at two locations with Coastal Riverine Group (CORIVGRU) 1 at San Diego and CORIVGRU 2 at Virginia Beach. At Virginia Beach there are two Active Component (AC) squadrons and two Reserve Component (RC) squadrons. At San Diego there is instead one AC Squadron and two RC squadrons. The requirement for a third Coastal Riverine Group to command and control the activities of riverine forces in the Persian Gulf saw the establishment of CORIVGRU 3 in 2014.

The Coastal Riverine Company (CRC) is the standard unit of action for the CRP. Each company is a highly mobile, quick to deploy and self contained unit that can operate independently or as part of a larger force. Each company has two platoons of personnel highly trained in all aspects of boarding vessels, search operations as well as intelligence gathering duties. Each CRC is equipped with four green water patrol boats and a further four riverine/harbour security boats.

The CRF operates six classes of patrol boats. For harbour patrol and escort of high value vessels the CRF has the 25 ft Oswald-class Tactical craft and the 34ft Force Protection - Large Patrol Boat. The heavily armed riverine boats include the 39ft Riverine Patrol Boat; 33ft Riverine Assault Boat and the 53ft Riverine Command Boat.

85' MkVI COMMAND BOAT

Machinery: Two MTU 16 V2000 M94 diesels; 5200 hp; Two Hamilton HM651 waterjets
Displacement: 46.6 tonnes **Dimensions:** 25.91m x 3.70m x 0.97m **Speed:** 35+ knots
Armament: Two Mk38 Mod2 25mm gun mounts; Four Kongsberg Sea Protector Mk50 stabilised small arms mounts; Six standard small arms mounts; Long Range Acoustic Device (LRAD) **Complement:** Two crews, five personnel in each, plus eight visit, Board, Search and Seizure (VBSS) personnel.

Notes: These vessels are designed to provide what is termed a persistent patrol in shallow water areas around the world including water just outside harbours and bays. Missions include the protection of high value naval assets and Board, Search and Seizure (VBSS) operations.

The Coastal Command Boat (CCB) is a 'one-off' prototype of the Mk VI, delivered to the Navy in 2013. At 65 feet (20m) long, it is somewhat smaller than the Mark VI. Its engine, armament, and other systems are otherwise identical to that of the Mark VI, though its smaller size gives it an endurance of over 24 hours at cruise speed. It was deployed to the US 5th Fleet in Bahrain in February 2014 to evaluate tactics and techniques for using the Mark VI in advance of the latter's deployment in 2015. It is assigned to Commander Task Group 56.7 of Commander Task Force 56.

RIVERINE COMMAND BOAT

Machinery: Two SAAB Scania diesels; Two Rolls-Royce waterjets; 850 hp
Displacement: 22.8 tonnes **Dimensions:** 15.1m x 3.78m x 0.9m **Speed:** 45 knots
Armament: One stabilised remotely operated mount on bridge roof; four fixed
gunmounts; Each mount capable of carrying either a Mk19 40mm Grenade Launcher;
Mk 44 GAU-17 mini-gun; 12.7mm MG; 7.62mm MG or 5.56mm MG **Complement:** 6 +
15 troops

Notes: These boats are licenced built by SAFE Boats International Washington and are
based on a Swedish design. The RCB is a highly flexible fully enclosed vessel that can
perform the tasks of command and control, fire support coordination, tactical mobility and
other tasks within littoral environments. The twin diesel engines provide immense
amounts of power that can drive these vessels through the water at speeds of up to 45
knots via their Rolls Royce waterjet propulsion systems.

RIVERINE ASSAULT BOAT

Machinery: Two turbo-charged Cummins diesel engines; 600 hp; Two waterjets **Displacement:** 7.4 tonnes **Dimensions:** 10.64m x 2.82m x 0.56m **Speed:** 40 knots **Armament:** Five positions for machine guns, Miniguns and grenade launchers **Complement:** 6 (plus up to 7 troops)

Notes: Of aluminium construction these vessels can be lifted out of the water and transported via road trailer when necessary. A dozen boats were acquired from US Marine Inc, Gulfport, between 2007-11.

RIVERINE PATROL BOAT

Machinery: Two Yanmar diesels; 880 hp; Two waterjets **Displacement:** 10.4 tonnes (FL) **Dimensions:** 12m x 3.1m x 0.61m **Speed:** 39 knots **Armament:** Three positions for machine guns and grenade launchers **Complement:** 2 (space for 16 troops)

Notes: These vessels are built from aluminium and have been extensively fitted with armour plating that provides some degree of protection against small arms and ballistic projectiles. The Riverine Patrol Boats are designed primarily for personnel transport and were built by SAFE Boats International. 24 boats were acquired between 2007-10.

34' FORCE PROTECTION BOAT

Machinery: Two Cummins diesels; 2 Konrad 520 drives or 2 Hamilton waterjets; 740 hp
Displacement: 9 tons **Dimensions:** 10.36m x 3.66m x 0.63m **Speed:** 36 knots
Armament: Four 12.7mm MG **Complement:** 6

Notes: These vessels are derived from SeaArk Marine's Dauntless design and are employed patrolling harbours and coastal areas. 134 craft were acquired with some deployed abroad protecting US military installations and forward operating bases.

A smaller class of 25' vessels called the Oswald Class built by SAFE Boats International with a rigid hull are also in service providing harbour surveillance, patrol and counter terrorism duties.

USS America

AMPHIBIOUS ASSAULT SHIPS (LHD/LHA) AMERICA CLASS

Ship	Hull Number	Completion Date	Builder
AMERICA	LHA 6	2014	H Ingalls SB
TRIPOLI	LHA 7	Building	H Ingalls SB
BOUGAINVILLE	LHA 8	On order	H Ingalls SB

Machinery: Two LM2500 gas turbines, two shafts, 72,000 shp, plus two 5,000 shp auxiliary propulsion motors **Displacement:** 45,693 tons full load **Dimensions:** 237.1m x 32.3m x 8.75m **Speed:** 20+ knots **Armament:** Two RAM launchers; two NATO Sea Sparrow launchers (with Evolved Sea Sparrow Missile (ESSM)); two 20mm Phalanx CIWS mounts; seven twin .50 cal. machine guns **Aircraft:** mix of AV-8B Harrier, F-35B Lightning II, MV-22B Osprey, CH-53E Super Stallion or CH-53K King Stallion, UH-1Y Venom, AH-1Z Viper, MH-60S Knighthawk **Complement:** 65 officers, 994 enlisted and 1,687 US Marines

Notes: The America Class evolved from the preceding Wasp Class and in particular the last of that class USS MAKIN ISLAND served as the basis of the America Class. The Flight O members of this new class of ships do, however, differ from the Wasp Class in not possessing a well deck for LCACs and other landing craft as well as having more limited hospital spaces in order to accommodate more aircraft and maintenance facilities. The wisdom of this approach has been questioned in many quarters and in fact the next ship of the class BOUGAINVILLE will return to the standard set in the Wasp and Tawara Classes of large American assault ships and see the restoration of the well deck at the stern of the ship. To make way for this LHA 8 will have less facilities for aircraft and aviation stores.

AMERICA and the follow on ships use a special hybrid engineering solution whereby the gas turbines are used for high speed transits whilst the diesel electric auxiliary engines are utilised when lower speeds are required. Interestingly the ship's gas turbines use the same JP-5 jet fuel as the embarked aircraft which greatly simplifies the storage and use of the fuels on board the ship. Typically each ship of the class could expect to operate a dozen MV-22B Osprey aircraft, six F-35B Lightning II, four CH-53K, seven AH-1Z/UK-1Y attack helicopters and a pair of MH-60S Knighthawk helicopters. The exact numbers will, obviously, vary according to the specified mission and could also include up to 20 AV-8B Harrier jump jets. The integration of the new F-35B Lightning II has not gone without a hitch as the jet blast from the aircraft has meant extra strengthening and special coatings have had to be applied to the flight deck due to the increased heat produced. TRIPOLI and BOUGAINVILLE will have these modifications added during their building process. BOUGAINVILLE will also differ from the two previous ships in having a slightly smaller design of island due to the addition of the well deck.

USS Boxer

AMPHIBIOUS ASSAULT
SHIPS (LHD/LHA)
WASP CLASS

Ship	Hull Number	Comm Date	Builder
WASP	LHD 1	1989	Ingalls SB
ESSEX	LHD 2	1992	Ingalls SB
KEARSARGE	LHD 3	1993	Ingalls SB
BOXER	LHD 4	1995	Ingalls SB
BATAAN	LHD 5	1997	Ingalls SB
BONHOMME RICHARD	LHD 6	1998	Ingalls SB
IWO JIMA	LHD 7	2001	Ingalls SB
MAKIN ISLAND	LHD 8	2007	Ingalls SB

Machinery: Two boilers; Two geared steam turbines driving two shafts; 70,000 shp
Displacement: 40,650 tons (LHD 1-4); 40,358 tons (LHD 5-7); 41,772 tons (LHD 8)
Dimensions: 240.2m x 32.3m x 8.1m **Speed:** 22 knots **Armament:** Two RAM launchers; two NATO Sea Sparrow launchers; three 20mm Phalanx CIWS mounts (two on LHD 5-7); four .50 cal. MG; four 25 mm Mk 38 MG (LHD 5-7 have three 25 mm Mk 38 MG) **Aircraft:** 12 MV-22 Osprey Tiltrotors; 4 CH-53E Sea Stallion helicopters; 6 AV-8B

Harrier attack aircraft; 3 UH-1N Huey helicopters; 4 AH-1W Super Cobra helicopters
Complement: 1,108 (+1,894 Marines)

Notes: The size of a small aircraft carrier these vessels are the largest amphibious ships in the US fleet capable of operating a wide range of V/STOL aircraft. Each of the ships has been designed to operate landing craft from a rear well dock which is large enough to accommodate up to three Landing Craft Air Cushion (LCAC) and other combinations of water craft. Each ship has extensive medical facilities with six operating theatres and a 600 bed hospital.

Usually these ships are deployed as part of an Expeditionary Strike Group (ESG) which traditionally comprises a LHD supported by LPDs and LSDs as well as escorting destroyers and cruisers.

Interestingly these were the last major units of the US Navy that were designed and built with steam propulsion. The last unit MAKIN ISLAND was, however, built with gas turbine engines.

USS Blue Ridge

AMPHIBIOUS COMMAND SHIPS BLUE RIDGE CLASS

Ship	Hull Number	Completion Date	Builder
BLUE RIDGE	LCC 19	1970	Philadelphia Naval SY
MOUNT WHITNEY	LCC 20	1971	Newport News SB

Machinery: Two boilers; one geared steam turbine driving one shaft; 22,000 shp **Displacement:** 18,874 tons **Dimensions:** 193.2m x 32.9m x 8.8m **Speed:** 23 knots **Armament:** 2 x Phalanx CIWS; 2 x 25mm Bushmaster cannons; 8.50 calibre M2 Browning MG **Complement:** 842 (with command staff embarked this rises to 268 officers and 1,173 enlisted)

Notes: This pair of ships was specially designed and built to serve as amphibious command ships with the necessary speed and size to accommodate all the command and control functions required during a complex amphibious operation. Both ships now serve as fleet flagships.

BLUE RIDGE is now the oldest deployable warship in the US fleet and in May 2018 completed a 23 month maintenance period that extended the ships, life for another twenty years that will mean when she finally retires from service the ship will be over 70 years old. The out of service date has now been set as 2039.

USS Green Bay

AMPHIBIOUS TRANSPORT
DOCK (LPD)
SAN ANTONIO CLASS

Ship	Hull Number	Completion Date	Builder
SAN ANTONIO	LPD 17	2006	Northrop Grumman/Avondale
NEW ORLEANS	LPD 18	2007	Northrop Grumman/Avondale
MESA VERDE	LPD 19	2007	Northrop Grumman/Pascagoula
GREEN BAY	LPD 20	2009	Northrop Grumman/Avondale
NEW YORK	LPD 21	2009	Northrop Grumman/Avondale
SAN DIEGO	LPD 22	2012	Northrop Grumman/Avondale
ANCHORAGE	LPD 23	2013	Northrop Grumman/Avondale
ARLINGTON	LPD 24	2013	Northrop Grumman/Pascagoula
SOMERSET	LPD 25	2014	Northrop Grumman/Avondale
JOHN P. MURTHA	LPD 26	*2016*	Northrop Grumman/Pascagoula
PORTLAND	LPD 27	*2017*	Northrop Grumman/Pascagoula
FORT LAUDERDALE	LPD 28	Building	Northrop Grumman/Pascagoula
RICHARD M. MCCOOL JR	LPD 29	Building	Northrop Grumman/Pascagoula

Machinery: Four sequentially turbo-charged marine Colt-Pielstick diesels driving two shafts; 41,600 shp **Displacement:** 25,300 tonnes **Dimensions:** 208.5m x 31.9m x 7m **Speed:** 22+ knots **Armament:** Two Bushmaster II 30mm Close in Guns; Two Rolling Airframe Missile launchers **Aircraft:** Launch or land two CH-53E Super Stallion helicopters or two MV-22 Osprey tilt-rotor aircraft or up to four CH-46 Sea Knight helicopters, AH-1 or UH-1 helicopters **Complement:** 360 (Embarked landing force 720 - surge capacity to 800)

Note: The San Antonio Class were designed and built to replace the elderly 1960s built Austin, Anchorage, Newport and Charleston-classes of amphibious shipping. The initial contract was awarded to Avondale Bath Alliance in December 1996. Following a contract dispute the contract was successfully resolved the following April. LPD 17 class workload was subsequently transferred to Northrop Grumman Ship Systems in June 2002.

These ships have 25,000 square feet of space for vehicles, 34,000 cubic feet for cargo and accommodation for up to 800 troops under surge capacity. The large aft well deck can accommodate LCAC vehicles that can carry men, equipment and stores ashore. The LP 17 class have excellent aviation facilities that include a hanger and a considerably larger (33%) flight deck than the preceding Austin Class. One notable feature of the San Antonio Class is the Advanced Enclosed Mast/Sensor (AEM/S). This structure has been designed to house the ship's radar and sensors within a shield to reduce signature/sensor maintenance.

A follow on class of ships to replace the Whidbey Island and Harpers Ferry-class LSDs was announced on 2 August 2018. The US Navy and Huntington Ingalls on that date signed a US$1.4 billion contract for long lead items for the construction of LPD30 the first of a 13 ship Flight II program. The new ships will be fitted with a Raytheon Enterprise Air Surveillance Radar, an upgrade over the existing AN/SPS-48 currently installled.

USS Ashland

WHIDBEY ISLAND CLASS

Ship	Hull Number	Completion Date	Builder
WHIDBEY ISLAND	LSD 41	1985	Lockheed SB & Construction Co
GERMANTOWN	LSD 42	1986	Lockheed SB & Construction Co
FORT McHENRY	LSD 43	1987	Lockheed SB & Construction Co
GUNSTON HALL	LSD 44	1989	Avondale Industries
COMSTOCK	LSD 45	1990	Avondale Industries
TORTUGA	LSD 46	1990	Avondale Industries
RUSHMORE	LSD 47	1991	Avondale Industries
ASHLAND	LSD 48	1992	Avondale Industries

Machinery: Four Colt Industries, 16 cylinder diesels driving two shafts; 33,000 shp **Displacement:** 15, 726 tonnes **Dimensions:** 185.6m x 25.6m x 6.3m **Speed:** 20+ knots **Armament:** Two 25mm Mk 38 Machine Guns; two 20mm Phalanx CIWS mounts and Six .50 cal MG, two Rolling Airframe (RAM) mounts **Landing Craft:** Four Landing Craft Air Cushion (LCAC) **Complement:** 22 officers, 391 enlisted (Marine Detachment 402 plus 302 surge)

Notes: The Whidbey Island-class of amphibious ships were designed and built around the use of the Landing Craft Air Cushion (LCAC) and currently hold the distinction of having the largest capacity for this type of vehicle of any US Navy warship (four). The stern of the ships are designed to flood to allow easy entry and exit from the vessel and can be flooded down within 15 minutes and reballast in 30 minutes. Once flooded the stern well has a depth of 6ft forward and 10 feet aft. The eight ships all have a large unobstructed flight deck positioned above the well dock with two landing spots for the largest of the US Navy's and US Marine Corps helicopters including the massive CH-53, but there is no hangerage available on board. The Whidbey Island-class ships can, however, fuel any visiting helicopters from the 90 tons of JP-5 aviation fuel they store on board. When designed the ships were equipped with extensive medical facilities including an operating room and a 8 bed hospital ward.

The second flight of San Antonio-class ships will eventually replace both the Whidbey Island and the Harpers Ferry-class ships in service.

USS Harpers Ferry

DOCK LANDING SHIP (LSD)
HARPERS FERRY CLASS

Ship	Hull Number	Commission Date	Builder
HARPERS FERRY	LSD 49	1995	Avondale Industries
CARTER HALL	LSD 50	1995	Avondale Industries
OAK HILL	LSD 51	1996	Avondale Industries
PEARL HARBOR	LSD 52	1998	Avondale Industries

Machinery: Four Colt Industries, 16 cylinder diesels driving two shaft; 33,000 shp **Displacement:** 16,976 tonnes **Dimensions:** 185.6m x 25.6m x 6.3m **Speed:** 20+ knots **Armament:** Two Rolling Air Frame (RAM) mounts, two 25mm Mk 38 MG; two 20mm Phalanx CIWS mounts and six .50 cal. MG **Landing Craft:** Two Landing Craft Air Cushion (LCAC) **Complement:** 419 (Marine Detachment 402 plus 102 surge)

Notes: Similar in design to Whidbey Island Class but were redesigned to serve in the cargo carrying role. The four ships of this class differ from the preceding class in only having space available to operate a pair of LCACs. The space this affords has instead been given over to the storage of cargoes needed by the Marine Corps. Other differences include a shortened well deck and the port side crane has also been removed.

These four ships will, in due course, be replaced by additional San Antonio-class units.

LCAC-63

LANDING CRAFT AIR CUSHION (LCAC)

Machinery: 4 x Allied-Signal TF-40B gas turbines (2 for propulsion/2 for lift); 16,000 hp sustained; 2 x shrouded reversible pitch airscrews; 4 x double-entry fans, centrifugal or mixed flow (lift); 4 x Vericor Power Systems ETF-40B gas turbines with Full Authority Digital Engine Control (FADEC) **Displacement:** 185 tonnes **Dimensions:** 26.4m x 14.3m **Speed:** 40+ knots **Armament:** 12.7mm MGs; Gun mounts will support: M2HB .50 cal machine gun; Mk 19 Mod3 40mm grenade launcher; M60 MG **Range:** 200 miles at 40 kts with payload / 300 miles at 35 kts with payload **Load:** 60 tons / 75 tons overload **Military Lift:** 24 troops or 1 Main Battle Tank **Complement:** 5

Notes: 91 LCACs were built between 1984 and 2001, production being split between two manufacturers Textron Marine and Land Systems and Avondale Gulfport Marine. The LCAC is a high speed, over the beach amphibious vehicle that can deliver a troop of soldiers, one Main Battle Tank or supplies up to 60-75 over the beach during an initial amphibious operation. The design of the LCAC with its air cushion technology allows it to access almost 70 percent of the world's coastline. Each of the LCACs that remain in service have received a Service Life Extension Program (SLEP) that extended their service lives from 20 to 30 years.

LANDING CRAFT
UTILITY (LCU) 1610 CLASS

Machinery: 2 x Detroit 12V-71 Diesel engines, twin shaft, 680 hp sustained, Kort nozzles **Displacement:** 381 tonnes **Dimensions:** 41.1m x 8.8m x 2m **Speed:** 12 knots **Armament:** 12.7mm MGs **Range:** 190 miles at 9 kts with full load **Load:** 180 tons **Military Lift:** 125 tons of cargo **Complement:** 14

Notes: These venerable landing craft are despite their advancing years, still extremely versatile and are being heavily used. LCUs are able to carry large amounts of cargoes, troops, tracked or wheeled vehicles from amphibious assault ships to beachheads or piers. They are equipped with bow and stern ramps to facilitate ease of transfer of cargoes. The LCU 1600 class vessels were built in large numbers from the 1960s to the 1980s and are used to transport large vehicles and cargoes too large for the LCACs to accommodate. Each LCU can carry up to 3 M-60 Main Battle Tanks or 400 troops.

Some of the LCUs in service are over 50 years old and the US Navy continues to look at options for their eventual replacement.

LANDING CRAFT UTILITY (LCU)
1627 & 1466 CLASS

Machinery: 3 x Gray Marine diesel engines; 3 shafts **Displacement:** 180 tons **Dimensions:** 35.08m x 10.36m x 1.83m **Speed:** 8 knots **Range:** 1,200 miles at 6 kts **Capacity:** 300 troops **Military Lift:** 170 tons **Complement:** 14

LCU 1466 Class
Machinery: 4 x Detroit diesel engines; 2 shafts **Displacement:** 392 tons **Dimensions:** 41.07m x 9.09m x 2.06m **Speed:** 8 knots **Range:** 1,200 miles at 6 kts **Capacity:** 350 troops **Military Lift:** 127 tons **Complement:** 12-14

Notes: The US Navy operates a fleet of landing craft including the LCU 1466 and LCU 1627 classes. These are self sustaining craft with accommodation on board for their crews. The craft have, over time, been adapted for a wide variety of uses within the US Navy including salvage operations, ferry boats and underwater test platforms. These vessels have bow ramps for onload/offload, and can be linked bow to stern gate to create a temporary pier-like structure. Its welded steel hull provides high durability with deck loads of 800 pounds per square foot. The design features two engine rooms separated by a watertight bulkhead to permit limited operation in the event that one engine room is disabled. An anchor system is installed on the starboard side aft to assist in retracting from the beach. These vessels are normally transported to their areas of operation onboard larger amphibious vessels such as LSDs and LHDs. The oldest vessels will start to be replaced under the Surface Connector (X) Recapitalization, or SC(X)R program.

USS Sea Fighter

EXPERIMENTAL CRAFT
SEA FIGHTER

Ship	Hull Number	Completion Date	Builder
SEA FIGHTER	FSF-1	2005	Nichols Brothers Boat Builders

Machinery: Two GE LM2500 Gas Turbines; two MTU diesels driving four Rolls-Royce waterjets **Displacement:** 950 tons **Dimensions:** 79.9m x 22m x 3.5m **Speed:** 50+ knots **Complement:** 26

Notes: On 5 February 2005 the Littoral Surface Craft-Experimental LSC(X) program was developed by the Office of Naval Research and was christened as SEA FIGHTER (FSF-1). This high speed vessel is constructed of aluminium and is of catamaran design. The ship tests a variety of technologies that will be incorporated into future ship designs of the US Navy. SEA FIGHTER operates out of San Diego under the control of USN's Third Fleet.

US NAVY / PM3 IAN W. ANDERSON   USS Frank Cable

SUBMARINE TENDERS
L.Y. SPEAR CLASS

Ship	Hull Number	Completion Date	Builder
EMORY S. LAND	AS 39	1979	Lockheed SB & Construction Co
FRANK CABLE	AS 40	1980	Lockheed SB & Construction Co

Machinery: Two boilers; two geared steam turbines driving one shaft; 20,000 shp
Displacement: 23,493 tons **Dimensions:** 196.2m x 25.9m x 8.7m **Speed:** 20 knots
Armament: Four 20mm Mk 67 Oerlikon **Complement:** 587 (plus 94 Flag Staff)

Notes: The L.Y. Spear Class was designed and equipped to support the US Navy's fleet
of nuclear powered submarines and four of these vessels can berth alongside each of
the ships at the same time. Each of these ships provides the submarines and their crews
with all essential maintenance and support including nuclear system repair and testing,
electronic and electrical repair, hull repair, sheet metal and steel work, pipe fabrication,
foundry, woodworking and hazardous materials management. The ships are also capable
of handling and storing submarine launched weapon systems as well as providing
accommodation for up to 1500 people. They each have one 30 tons crane and a pair of
mobile cranes.

USNS Grasp

RESCUE AND SALVAGE VESSEL
SAFEGUARD CLASS

Ship	Hull Number	Completion Date	Builder
GRASP	T-ARS 51	1985	Peterson
SALVOR	T-ARS 52	1986	Peterson

Machinery: Four Caterpillar 299 Diesels, two shafts, 4,200 hp **Displacement:** 3,200 tons **Dimensions:** 77.7m x 15.2m x 4.7m **Speed:** 15 knots **Complement:** 26 (plus 4 US Navy)

Notes: These ships are the survivors of a class of four such vessels that were built in the mid 1980s to perform rescue and salvage operations on behalf of the US Navy. They were in 2006 transferred to the Maritime Sealift Command. Each ship is equipped with four foam firefighting monitors and can operate ROVs. SALVOR is based at Pearl Harbor, Hawaii and GRASP is homeported at Norfolk, Virginia.

YARD PATROL CRAFT YP-703 CLASS

Machinery: Two Caterpillar C-18 diesels driving two shafts; 1,400 bhp **Displacement:** 228 tons FL **Dimensions:** 36.3m x 8.51m x 2.27m **Speed:** 12.6 knots **Complement:** 4 (plus 6 Trainees/Midshipmen; accommodation for 30)

Notes: Built by C & G Boatworks, Mobile, Alabama, construction of this class of small yard patrol craft commenced in 2010. They were designed to improve habitability, training areas, manoeuvrability, propulsion plant and have an integrated bridge. They were also equipped for simulated Underway Replenishment although not able to actually undertake such manoeuvres. The hulls are built from steel with aluminium superstructures and are based at the US Naval Academy in Annapolis in Maryland.

YARD PATROL CRAFT YP-676 CLASS

Machinery: Two Detroit 12V-71 diesels driving two shafts; 680 shp **Displacement:** 167 tons FL **Dimensions:** 32.9m x 7.3m x 2.4m **Speed:** 13 knots **Complement:** 6 (plus 24 Trainees/Midshipmen)

Notes: In the 1980s 23 similar yard patrol craft were built of which sixteen remain active in 2019. These craft are used for training and research purposes with trainees and midshipman being taught a range of nautical skills such as navigation, damage control and seamanship. YP 676, 681, 683, 684, 686-692, 694, 695, 698, 700 are used at the US Naval Academy, Annapolis, MD, whilst 701 is used at the Naval Undersea Warfare Centre in Keyport Washington.

USS Constitution

HISTORIC FLAGSHIP

Ship	Completion Date	Builder
CONSTITUTION	1797	Edmond Hartt's Shipyard, Boston

Propulsion: 42,710 sq. ft of sail on three masts **Displacement:** 2,200 tons **Dimensions:** 62m (53m at waterline) x 13.3m x 4.4m **Speed:** 13+ knots **Complement:** 450 including 55 Marines and 30 boys (1797)

Notes: USS CONSTITUTION is the world's oldest commissioned warship still afloat. The term flagship is bestowed on this vessel although it is in name only as she holds no official flagship status. Today 'Old Ironsides' as she is affectionately known acts in the capacity of the USN's ambassador to the public. She is based in Boston and is usually open to the public. The ship has a crew of 55 active duty USN crewmembers who maintain the ship as well as 25 Navy employed civilians.

In 2014 she received a major three year US$15 million restoration program at the Charlestown Navy Yard that saw the ship dry docked and refurbished from stem to stern. On 23 July 2017 she completed the restoration work and returned to her usual place at the Navy Yard Pier.

AUXILIARY PERSONNEL LIGHT - SMALL (APLS)

Displacement: 2,744 tons   **Dimensions:** 81.99m x 21.03m x 1.57m   **Complement:** 600
Food Service Capability: 1130 personnel

Notes: In late 2018 VT Halter Marine were awarded a US$77.9 million contract to design and construct the APL(S)-67 class of barracks ships for the US Navy. Based on commercial designs provided to the oil and gas industry these vessels can accommodate the crew of a single Nimitz-class aircraft carrier for short periods or whilst ships are in port for availabilities and Inter-Deployment Training Cycles (IDTC). Of the current barracks ships thirteen of the seventeen were built between 1944-1946 and are becoming increasingly hard to maintain and modernise.

Each of the new APL(S)s will have around 600 berths and messing arrangements for 1,100 personnel. These craft have no motive power of their own and will be towed from location to location as required.

The initial order for VT Halter Marine is for two barges with an expected completion date of July 2020. The US Navy has options for another four vessels of the same class, which could be worth US$244 million to VT Halter Marine. APL(S)s will replace the older barges, which are located around US Navy bases including Norfolk and Portsmouth, San Diego, Bremerton, Mayport, Pearl Harbor, Yokosuka, Sasebo and Guam.

USS Battle Point

TORPEDO RECOVERY/TRIALS VESSELS
CAPE FLATTERY CLASS

Ship	Hull Number	Completion Date	Builder
BATTLE POINT	YTT 10	1991	McDermott Shipyard, Morgan City
DISCOVERY BAY	YTT 11	1992	McDermott Shipyard, Morgan City

Machinery: 1 Cummins KTA50-M diesel; 1,250hp; one shaft; one bow thruster; two stern thrusters **Displacement:** 1,168 tons **Dimensions:** 57m x 12m x 3.4m **Speed:** 11 knots **Complement:** 31

Notes: These vessels serve in the role of torpedo recovery and trials vessels supporting the submarine service during live fire exercises and conducting research into torpedo technology. Both vessels are based at Keyport.

DEEP SUBMERGE VEHICLE

Ship	Hull Number	Completion Date	Builder
CUTTHROAT	LSV-2	2001	Newport News Shipbuilding

Machinery: Permanent Magnet Electric Motor; one shaft **Displacement:** Classified **Dimensions:** 33.8m x 10m x 10m **Speed:** 34 knots **Diving depth:** Classified **Complement:** Unmanned

Notes: This trials vessel is a quarter scale version of the Virginia-class attack submarines. It is the world's largest autonomous unmanned submarine and is used to test advanced submarine concepts for the US Navy. The submarine was built by Newport News Shipbuilding (40 percent) and General Dynamics/Electric Boat (35 percent). Other partners included GNB Technologies (propulsion batteries), Naval Surface Warfare Center (Onboard Data Acquisition System), Lockheed Martin (Guidance, Navigation, and Control System), Vehicle Control Technologies (Guidance, Navigation, and Control System), Allied Signal (Electro-Mechanical Hydraulic Actuators), and Eaton (Electric Drive Control System). She is operated on Lake Pend Oreille in Idaho under the operation of the Naval Surface Warfare Center's Carderock Division.

ELECTRIC SHIP DEMONSTRATOR

Ship	Hull Number	Completion Date	Builder
SEA JET	AESD	2005	Dakota Creek Industries

Machinery: 1 General Dynamics RIMJET Integrated Motor Propulsor; 800hp **Displacement:** 122 tons FL **Dimensions:** 41m x 14.1m x 5.9m **Speed:** 8 knots (diesel) 16 knots (electric) **Complement:** 3

Notes: Built to support the Zumwalt-class destroyer as seen by her distinctive tumble-home hull design, this vessel continues to provide valuable information and data about electric drive propulsion for future US Naval vessels. She is operated out of the Carderock Division's Acoustic Research Detachment in Bayview, Idaho.

EXPERIMENTAL SWATH (AGE)

Ship	Hull Number	Completion Date	Builder
STILLETO	---	2006	M Ship Co

Machinery: 4 Caterpillar diesels; 6,000hp, 4 surface piercing propellers **Displacement:** 61 tons FL **Dimensions:** 26.82m x 12.19m x 0.91m **Speed:** 50 knots **Complement:** 35 **Aircraft:** Platform for 2 SH-60R helicopters

Notes: This vessel is a stealth prototype developed by the M Ship Company as a demonstrator of new technologies. The ship features an advanced Pentamaran hull design and is constructed of sophisticated carbon fibre and other composite materials.

AUXILIARY FLOATING DRY DOCKS

Small Auxiliary Floating Dry Dock

Name	Hull Number	Completion Date	Location
DYNAMIC	AFDL 6	1944	Norfolk, Virginia

Medium Auxiliary Floating Dry Dock

Name	Hull Number	Completion Date	Location
SHIPPING PORT	ARDM 4	1979	---
ARGO	ARDM 5	1986	---

Notes: The US Navy at one time had the largest collection of floating dry docks in the world. Over the last thirty years these have declined either by sale to foreign or domestic new owners or by scrapping. Currently the US Navy owns and operates the above floating dry docks.

EXPERIMENTAL CRAFT SEA HUNTER

Ship	Hull Number	Completion Date	Builder
SEA HUNTER	---	2016	Vigor Industries
SEA HUNTER II	---	Building	Leidos Inc., Reston

Machinery: 2 x diesel engines driving twin propellers **Displacement:** 145 tons FL **Dimensions:** 40m **Speed:** 27 knots **Range:** 10,000 nautical miles **Armament:** None **Complement:** None

Notes: SEA HUNTER is the culmination of the DARPA inspired Anti Submarine Warfare Continuous Trail Unmanned Vessel (ACTUV) program. She was christened on 7 April 2016 and is designated in the US Navy as the Medium Displacement Unmanned Surface Vehicle (MDUSV). SEA HUNTER cost US$20 million to build and was designed as a 40m long trimaran hull with two outriggers. Her 14,000 gallons of diesel are enough to allow the craft to travel between San Diego to Guam and back to Pearl Harbour on a single tank. The craft has the ability to be fitted with a crew compartment if necessary but usually computers will control and drive the ship with minimal human oversight in a concept called Sparse Supervisory Control. The computer on board uses optical guidance and radar to avoid obstacles. SEA HUNTER completed her sea trials and is now being accessed by the Office of Naval Research for roles such as mine countermeasures and submarine detection. Plans exist to fit the craft with intelligence, surveillance and reconnaissance equipment and offensive anti-submarine payloads. If the trials are successful within ten years this type of vessel could replace destroyers on secondary missions within the US Navy. The second vessel of the class was ordered on 15 December 2017.

SEABASE TO SHORE CONNECTOR

Machinery: 4 x Rolls Royce MT7 gas turbines **Displacement:** 87.2 tons **Dimensions:** 26.4m x 14.3m **Speed:** 40+ knots **Range:** 200 miles at 40 knots/300 miles at 35 knots **Armament:** 2 x 12.7mm machine guns, Gun mounts can support the M2HB .50cal machine gun; Mk19 Mod 3 40mm grenade launcher, or the M60 machine gun **Load:** 73 tonnes **Complement:** 5

Notes: The Ship to Shore Connector (SSC) or LCAC-100 program is an evolutionary program that takes the very best of the existing LCAC air cushion vehicles and maximises the potential for future growth. Based on the existing size and dimensions of the LCAC in order to fit within the well docks of amphibious shipping the LCAC-100 program will replace 73 of the LCACs by 2032 when the program is due for completion and existing heritage LCAC vehicles will have been retired from service.

SSC will offer the USN and USMC improved performance from the four Rolls Royce MT7 gas turbines which have been developed from those used in the USMC's fleet of Osprey tilt rotor aircraft. The new vehicles will offer increased cargo and personnel carrying capabilities over existing LCACs with a target of 145 combat equipped Marines or 108 casualties.

LCAC-100 is the first 'in house' designed program for more than 15 years. The contract for the construction of the vehicles was awarded to Textron Inc of New Orleans and the first vehicles in a production run of 73 projected vehicles was delivered in 2018. Initial Operational Capability is expected sometime in 2020.

SMALL INSHORE CRAFT
2 + 1 SEALION INSERTION CRAFT

Machinery: 2 MTU 10V2000 M93 diesels; 3,900hp; 2 Karnewa waterjets
Displacement: 34 tons FL **Speed:** 52 knots **Range:** 400 nautical miles at 40 knots
Armament: 2 x 12.7mm Remote Controlled guns

Notes: The Combatant Craft Heavy SEAL Insertion, Observation and Neutralization (SEALION) has as its primary role the long range insertion and extraction of US Navy SEAL teams from combat zones in the littoral. The vessels were built by Vigor Works with the first prototype first commencing trials in 2003. Funding for a third vessel was approved in June 2017 and the vessel is expected to enter service in 2019. Operational capability is expected sometime in 2020.

SMALL INSHORE CRAFT
The US Navy maintains a large fleet of small craft for inshore work ranging in size from small workboats, inflatables to larger patrol craft. This number fluctuates from year to year but at the time of writing (December 2018) comprised the following:

41 x 28ft Patrol Craft
50 x 27ft Patrol Craft
60 x 11 Metre RIB
118 x 34ft Patrol Craft
18 x 25ft Patrol Craft
30 x Combatant Craft Assault

MILITARY SEALIFT COMMAND

In the Second World War essential supplies and support for US Navy operations was conducted by four separate agencies which at times was confusing. In 1949 these different aspects came under one all encompassing umbrella with the founding of the Military Sea Transportation Service, the forerunner of today's Military Sea Lift Command (renamed in 1970). The Military Sea Lift Command is now responsible for managing the Department of Defense's ocean transportation needs.

Military Sea Lift Command is a massive operation with almost 11,000 employees worldwide of which 80 percent serve aboard the large fleet of ships, which are all civilian manned. The Command is broken down into specialist forces: Combat Logistic Force, Service Support Program, Special Mission Program, Strategic Sealift Program and Ready Reserve Force.

COMBAT LOGISTICS FORCE
The first of these specialist forces began in 1972 as the Naval Fleet Auxiliary Force and provides the US Navy with fuel, food, ordnance, spare parts, mail and other critical supplies that enable the US Navy to remain at sea and combat ready at all times. Under this command are found the large Henry J. Kaiser-class tankers, the Lewis and Clark-class dry cargo/ammunition ships and the Supply-class Fast Combat Ships.

SERVICE SUPPORT PROGRAM
The Service Support Program provides the US Navy with support when it comes to operational towing, rescue and salvage operations as well as miscellaneous tasks such as cable laying, submarine support and repairs. Special Mission Program currently operates a fleet of approximately 24 unique vessels in support of federal government missions and a variety of specialist US military taskings such as intelligence gathering, hydrographic surveys, missile tracking and submarine support. The Special Mission Program also manages Harbour Tug Services on behalf of Navy Installations Command around the Continental USA and Hawaii, Alaska and Guam.

STRATEGIC SEALIFT PROGRAM
The Strategic Sealift Program is the result of a 2014 merger between the Prepositioning and Sealift Programs where military equipment and supplies are positioned at strategic locations around the world onboard ships in readiness for any eventuality. Supplies and equipment could be from any of the main services (Air Force, Army, Marine Corps and Defense Logistic Agency). The placing of large supplies of military equipment ensures that commanders in the field know that operations can commence quickly where ever and whenever necessary.

READY RESERVE FORCE
The final segment of the Sealift Command's remit is the Ready Reserve Force which is owned and managed by the US Maritime Administration. Essentially these are ships which are kept in good working order at strategic locations to ensure that there is

sufficient shipping available to satisfy any surge requirements. The decline of the US merchant fleet across the last fifty years has meant that these ships held in reserve have become increasingly necessary. The fleet comprises a wide variety of vessels ranging from crane ships, ro-ro ferries, heavy lift ships and fuel tankers. Depending on the ship they are maintained at four, five, ten or twenty days readiness to sail on a mission.

SHIPS OF THE MILITARY SEALIFT COMMAND

Ship	Hull Number	Ship	Hull Number
COMBAT LOGISTICS FORCE			T-AKE 11
		WILLIAM McLEAN	T-AKE 12
Fast Combat Support Ship		MEDGAR EVERS	T-AKE 13
		CESAR CHAVEZ	T-AKE 14
SUPPLY	T-AOE 6		
ARCTIC	T-AOE 8	**SERVICE SUPPORT**	
Fleet Replenishment Oiler		**Hospital Ship**	
HENRY J. KAISER	T-AO 187	MERCY	T-AH 19
JOSHUA HUMPHREYS	T-AO 188	COMFORT	T-AH 20
JOHN LENTHALL	T-AO 189		
WALTER S. DIEHL	T-AO 193	**Rescue-Salvage Ship**	
JOHN ERICSSON	T-AO 194		
LEROY GRUMMAN	T-AO 195	GRASP	T-ARS 51
KANAWHA	T-AO 196	SALVOR	T-ARS 52
PECOS	T-AO 197		
BIG HORN	T-AO 198	**Fleet Ocean Tug**	
TIPPECANOE	T-AO 199		
GUADALUPE	T-AO 200	CATAWBA	T-ATF 168
PATUXENT	T-AO 201	SIOUX	T-ATF 171
YUKON	T-AO 202	APACHE	T-ATF 172
LARAMIE	T-AO 203		
RAPPAHANNOCK	T-AO 204	**Cable Repair Ship**	
Dry Cargo/Ammunition Ship		ZEUS	T-ARC 7
LEWIS AND CLARK	T-AKE 1	**Expeditionary Fast Transport**	
SACAGAWEA	T-AKE 2		
ALAN SHEPARD	T-AKE 3	SPEARHEAD	T-EPF 1
RICHARD E. BYRD	T-AKE 4	CHOCKTAW COUNTY	T-EPF 2
ROBERT E. PEARY	T-AKE 5	MILLINOCKET	T-EPF 3
AMELIA EARHART	T-AKE 6	FALL RIVER	T-EPF 4
CARL BRASHEAR	T-AKE 7	TRENTON	T-EPF 5
WALLY SCHIRRA	T-AKE 8	BRUNSWICK	T-EPF 6
MATTHEW PERRY	T-AKE 9	CARSON CITY	T-EPF 7
CHARLES DREW	T-AKE 10	YUMA	T-EPF 8
WASHINGTON CHAMBERS			

Ship	Hull Number	Ship	Hull Number
CITY OF BISMARCK	T-EPF 9	ABLE	T-AGOS 20
BURLINGTON	T-EPF 10	EFFECTIVE	T-AGOS 21
PUERTO RICO	T-EPF 11	LOYAL	T-AGOS 22
NEWPORT	T-EPF 12	IMPECCABLE	T-AGOS 23
Unnamed	T-EPF 13		
Unnamed	T-EPF 14		

Submarine & Special Warfare Support Vessel

SSV C-CHAMPION
SSV C-COMMANDO
MV DOLORES CHOUEST
MV HOS ARROWHEAD
MV HOS BLACK POWDER
MV HOS DOMINATOR
MV HOS EAGLE VIEW
MV HOS WESTWIND
MV MALAMA

SPECIAL MISSION SHIPS

Sea Base X-Band Radar

SBX-1	SBX-1

Missile Range Instrumentation Ship

INVINCIBLE	T-AGM 24
HOWARD O. LORENZEN	T-AGM 25

STRATEGIC SEALIFT SHIPS

LMSR

Oceanographic Survey Ship

PATHFINDER	T-AGS 60
SUMNER	T-AGS 61
BOWDITCH	T-AGS 62
HENSON	T-AGS 63
BRUCE C. HEEZEN	T-AGS 64
MARY SEARS	T-AGS 65
MAURY	T-AGS 66
NEIL ARMSTRONG	AGOR 27
SALLY RIDE	AGOR 28

SHUGHART	T-AKR 295
GORDON	T-AKR 296
YANO	T-AKR 297
GILLILAND	T-AKR 298
BOB HOPE	T-AKR 300
FISHER	T-AKR 301
SEAY	T-AKR 302
MENDONCA	T-AKR 303
PILILAAU	T-AKR 304
BRITTIN	T-AKR 305
BENAVIDEZ	T-AKR 306
WATSON	T-AKR 310
SISLER	T-AKR 311
DAHL	T-AKR 312
RED CLOUD	T-AKR 313
CHARLTON	T-AKR 314
WATKINS	T-AKR 315

Navigation Test Support Ship

WATERS	T-AGS 45

Ocean Surveillance Ship

VICTORIOUS	T-AGOS 19

Ship	Hull Number	Ship	Hull Number
POMEROY	T-AKR 316		
SODERMAN	T-AKR 317		

Container & Roll-on/Roll-off Ships

Ship	Hull Number
SGT MATEJ KOCAK	T-AK 3005
PFC EUGENE A. O'BREGON	T-AK 3006
MAJ STEPHEN W. PLESS	T-AK 3007
2ND LT JOHN P. BOBO	T-AK 3008
PFC DEWAYNE T. WILLIAMS	T-AK 3009
1ST LT BALDOMERO LOPEZ	T-AK 3010
1ST LT JACK LUMMUS	T-AK 3011
SGT WILLIAM R. BUTTON	T-AK 3012
1ST LT HARRY L. MARTIN	T-AK 3015
LCPL ROY M. WHEAT	T-AK 3016
GYSGT FRED W. STOCKHAM	T-AK 3017

Container Ships

Ship	Hull Number
TSGT JOHN A. CHAPMAN	T-AK 323
MAJ BERNARD F. FISHER	T-AK 4396
LTC JOHN U. D. PAGE	T-AK 4543
SSGT EDWARD A. CARTER	T-AK 4544

Government-owned Tanker

Ship	Hull Number
LAWRENCE H. GIANELLA	T-AOT 1125

Long Term Government Charter

Ship	Hull Number
MV MOHEGAN	T-AK 5158
MV BBC SEATTLE	T-AK 5272
MT EMPIRE STATE	T-AOT 5193
MT EVERGREEN STATE	T-AOT 5205
MV MAERSK PEARY	T-AOT 5246

High-Speed Vessel

Ship	Hull Number
GUAM	T-HST-1

Mobile Landing Platform Ship

Ship	Hull Number
MONTFORD POINT	T-ESD 1
JOHN GLENN	T-ESD 2
LEWIS B. PULLER	T-ESB 3
HERSCHEL 'WOODY' WILLIAMS	T-ESB 4
MIGUEL KEITH	T-ESB 5
---	T-ESB 6

Aviation Maintenance Logistics Ships

Ship	Hull Number
WRIGHT	T-AVB 3
CURTISS	T-AVB 4

Offshore Petroleum Delivery Ship

Ship	Hull Number
VADM K. R. WHEELER	T-AG 5001

READY RESERVE FORCE SHIPS

Fast Sealift Ship

Ship	Hull Number
ALGOL	T-AKR 287

Ship	Hull Number	Ship	Hull Number
BELLATRIX	T-AKR 288	**Heavy Lift Ships**	
DENEBOLA	T-AKR 289		
POLLUX	T-AKR 290	CAPE MAY	T-AKR 5063
ALTAIR	T-AKR 291	CAPE MOHICAN	T-AKR 5065
REGULUS	T-AKR 292		
CAPELLA	T-AKR 293	**Crane Ships**	
ANTARES	T-AKR 294		
		KEYSTONE STATE	T-ACS 1
		GEM STATE	T-ACS 2
Roll-on/Roll-off Ships		GRAND CANYON STATE	
			T-ACS 3
CAPE ISLAND	T-AKR 10	GOPHER STATE	T-ACS 4
CAPE INTREPID	T-AKR 11	FLICKERTAIL STATE	T-ACS 5
CAPE TEXAS	T-AKR 112	CORNHUSKER STATE	T-ACS 6
CAPE TAYLOR	T-AKR 113		
ADM Wm. M. CALLAGHAN			
	T-AKR 1001		
CAPE ORLANDO	T-AKR 2044		
CAPE DUCATO	T-AKR 5051		
CAPE DOUGLAS	T-AKR 5052		
CAPE DOMINGO	T-AKR 5053		
CAPE DECISION	T-AKR 5054		
CAPE DIAMOND	T-AKR 5055		
CAPE ISABEL	T-AKR 5062		
CAPE HUDSON	T-AKR 5066		
CAPE HENRY	T-AKR 5067		
CAPE HORN	T-AKR 5068		
CAPE EDMONT	T-AKR 5069		
CAPE INSCRIPTION	T-AKR 5076		
CAPE KNOX	T-AKR 5082		
CAPE KENNEDY	T-AKR 5083		
CAPE VINCENT	T-AKR 9666		
CAPE RISE	T-AKR 9678		
CAPE RAY	T-AKR 9679		
CAPE VICTORY	T-AKR 9701		
CAPE TRINITY	T-AKR 9711		
CAPE RACE	T-AKR 9960		
CAPE WASHINGTON	T-AKR 9961		
CAPE WRATH	T-AKR 9962		

USNS Arctic

COMBAT LOGISTICS FORCE
FAST COMBAT SUPPORT SHIPS
SUPPLY CLASS

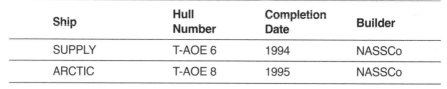

Ship	Hull Number	Completion Date	Builder
SUPPLY	T-AOE 6	1994	NASSCo
ARCTIC	T-AOE 8	1995	NASSCo

Machinery: Four GE LM2500 gas turbines driving two shafts; 105,000 shp
Displacement: 49,583 tonnes **Dimensions:** 229.9m x 32m x 11.6m **Speed:** 25 knots
Aircraft: 3 x Medium helicopters **Complement:** 160 civilians (50 military)

Notes: Transferred from the USN between 2001-04, these two ships are the last survivors of a class of four, RAINIER and BRIDGE having been placed in reserve. They are the largest combat logistic ships currently operated by the MSC. The Supply Class are capable of speeds that allow them to operate alongside carrier groups and are able to resupply fuel, lubricants, oils, dry stores and ammunition.

USNS Rappahannock

FLEET REPLENISHMENT OILER HENRY J. KAISER CLASS

Ship	Hull Number	Completion Date	Builder
HENRY J. KAISER	T-AO 187	1986	Avondale
JOSHUA HUMPHREYS	T-AO 188	1987	Avondale
JOHN LENTHALL	T-AO 189	1987	Avondale
WALTER S. DIEHL	T-AO 193	1988	Avondale
JOHN ERICSSON	T-AO 194	1991	Avondale
LEROY GRUMMAN	T-AO 195	1989	Avondale
KANAWHA	T-AO 196	1991	Avondale
PECOS	T-AO 197	1990	Avondale
BIG HORN	T-AO 198	1992	Avondale
TIPPECANOE	T-AO 199	1993	Avondale
GUADALUPE	T-AO 200	1992	Avondale
PATUXENT	T-AO 201	1995	Avondale
YUKON	T-AO 202	1993	Avondale

Ship	Hull Number	Completion Date	Builder
LARAMIE	T-AO 203	1996	Avondale
RAPPAHANNOCK	T-AO 204	1995	Avondale

Machinery: 2 Colt-Pielstick 10 PC4.2 V 570 diesels driving 2 shafts; Controllable Pitch propellers **Displacement:** 42,674 tonnes **Dimensions:** 206.5m x 29.7m x 4m **Speed:** 20 knots **Complement:** 66-89 civilian (7-24 military)

Notes: This class of oiler have stations on either beam for underway replenishment for fuel and stores. The class also has a small capacity for the storage and transfer of fresh and frozen foods.

The first nine ships of the class were named after famous American industrialists, shipbuilders, inventors, naval architects and aeronautical engineers. The remaining ten ships were named after American rivers.

PATUXENT, RAPPAHANNOCK and LARAMIE's construction was delayed by the decision to fit the ships with double hulls in order to conform with the Oil Pollution Act of 1990. This modification increased construction time from 32 to 42 months and reduced fuel capacity by 17 percent, although this can be restored in an emergency. Hull separation is 1.83m at the sides and 1.98m at the bottom.

Two vessels, BENJAMIN ISHERWOOD (T-AO 191) and HENRY ECKFORD (T-AO 192), were sent for long term lay up when only 95% and 83% complete. Both were subsequently towed to Brownsville, Texas, in 2011 for breaking up without ever being completed.

USNS Cesar Chavez

AUXILIARY DRY CARGO SHIPS

LEWIS AND CLARK CLASS

Ship	Hull Number	Completion Date	Builder
LEWIS AND CLARK	T-AKE 1	2006	GD NASSCO
SACAGAWEA	T-AKE 2	2007	GD NASSCO
ALAN SHEPARD	T-AKE 3	2007	GD NASSCO
RICHARD E. BYRD	T-AKE 4	2007	GD NASSCO
ROBERT E. PEARY	T-AKE 5	2008	GD NASSCO
AMELIA EARHART	T-AKE 6	2008	GD NASSCO
CARL BRASHEAR	T-AKE 7	2009	GD NASSCO
WALLY SCHIRRA	T-AKE 8	2009	GD NASSCO
MATTHEW PERRY	T-AKE 9	2010	GD NASSCO
CHARLES DREW	T-AKE 10	2010	GD NASSCO
WASHINGTON CHAMBERS	T-AKE 11	2011	GD NASSCO
WILLIAM McLEAN	T-AKE 12	2011	GD NASSCO
MEDGAR EVERS	T-AKE 13	2012	GD NASSCO

Ship	Hull Number	Completion Date	Builder
CESAR CHAVEZ	T-AKE 14	2012	GD NASSCO

Machinery: Integrated propulsion and ship service electrical distribution system; four FM/MAN diesel generators with total installed power of 35.7 MW. Twin synchronous, variable speed, reversible, double wound, Alstom propulsion motors mounted in tandem, single fixed-pitch propeller **Displacement:** 40,945 tons **Dimensions:** 210m x 32.31m x 9m **Speed:** 20 knots **Complement:** 123 civilian (plus 49 military)

Notes: Built as replacements for the Kilauea, Sacramento, Mars and Sirius-class tankers and combat stores ships. These ships are capable of delivering ammunition, provisions, stores, spare parts, potable water and petroleum products to carrier strike groups and other naval forces worldwide.

The ships in the class are named after famous American explorers and pioneers.

US NAVY/MCS3 SARAH MYERS   USNS Wally Schirra

USNS Comfort

SERVICE SUPPORT
HOSPITAL SHIPS

Ship	Hull Number	Completion Date	Conversion
MERCY	T-AH 19	1986	NASSCO SD
COMFORT	T-AH 20	1987	NASSCO SD

Machinery: 2 GE turbines; two boilers; one shaft **Displacement:** 70,473 tonnes **Dimensions:** 272.6m x 32.2m x 10m **Speed:** 17 knots **Complement:** 63 (plus 956 naval medical staff and 258 naval support staff).

Notes: Both ships started their careers as San Clemente-class super tankers before being converted by NASSCO shipyard at San Diego into hospital ships for the MSC. These ships are usually kept in a reduced state of operational readiness but can be brought back into service at five days notice. Each ship contains 12 fully equipped operating rooms, a 1,000 bed hospital, digital radiological services, a medical laboratory, a pharmacy, an optometry lab, a CAT scan and two oxygen producing plants. Each ship has a helicopter landing deck capable of accommodating the largest military helicopters in Allied service. There are also side ports in the hull to allow the transfer of patients at sea.

USNS Apache

FLEET OCEAN TUGS
POWHATAN CLASS

Ship	Hull Number	Completion Date	Builder
CATAWBA	T-ATF 168	1980	Marinette Marine
SIOUX	T-ATF 171	1981	Marinette Marine
APACHE	T-ATF 172	1981	Marinette Marine

Machinery: 2 GM EMD 20-645F7B diesels driving 2 shafts; Kort nozzles; controllable pitch props; bow thruster **Displacement:** 2,296.27 tons **Dimensions:** 73.2m x 12.8m x 4.6m **Speed:** 14.5 knots **Complement:** 16 civilians (four naval communicators)

Notes: Fleet tugs used to tow ships, barges and targets for gunnery exercises. They are also extremely versatile vessels used for a wide variety of tasks including salvage, diving and rescue work. Each tug is equipped with a 10 tons capacity crane and has a bollard pull of at least 87 tons. There are two GPH fire pumps supplying three fire monitors able to produce up to 2,200 gallons of foam per minute. NAVAJO (T-ATF 169) was decommissioned in October 2016.

USNS Zeus

CABLE REPAIR SHIP

Ship	Hull Number	Completion Date	Builder
ZEUS	T-ARC 7	1984	NASSCo

Machinery: Diesel-electric, twin shaft, 12,200 shp **Displacement:** 14,384.19 tons
Dimensions: 153.2m x 22.3m x 7.6m **Speed:** 15 knots **Complement:** 54 civilians, 27 military/sponsor.

Notes: This is the first cable repair ship designed and built as such for the US Navy, previous ships in the role having been refitting from other designations. The two principal roles of ZEUS are oceanography and the installation and maintenance of submarine cable systems. The vessel is equipped with a wide range of equipment for these tasks including five cable tanks, cable transporters, cable tension machines, self fleeting cable drums, overboarding sheaves and a dynamometer cable fairleader. She is also fitted with both single beam and multi-beam sonars for bottom profiling. ZEUS is capable of laying 1,000 miles of cable in depths of up to 9,000 feet before having to return to shore to replenish her cable stocks. She is based on the Atlantic coast and spends an average of 300 days at sea annually.

USNS Carson City

EXPEDITIONARY FAST
TRANSPORT

Ship	Hull Number	Commission Date	Builder
SPEARHEAD	T-EPF 1	2012	Bollinger/IncatUSA
CHOCKTAW COUNTY	T-EPF 2	2013	Bollinger/IncatUSA
MILLINOCKET	T-EPF 3	2014	Bollinger/IncatUSA
FALL RIVER	T-EPF 4	2014	Bollinger/IncatUSA
TRENTON	T-EPF 5	2015	Bollinger/IncatUSA
BRUNSWICK	T-EPF 6	2016	Bollinger/IncatUSA
CARSON CITY	T-EPF 7	2016	Bollinger/IncatUSA
YUMA	T-EPF 8	2017	Bollinger/IncatUSA
CITY OF BISMARCK	T-EPF 9	2017	Bollinger/IncatUSA
BURLINGTON	T-EPF 10	Building	Bollinger/IncatUSA
PUERTO RICO	T-EPF 11	Building	Bollinger/IncatUSA
NEWPORT	T-EPF 12	Building	Bollinger/IncatUSA
UNNAMED	T-EPF 13	Ordered	Bollinger/IncatUSA
UNNAMED	T-EPF 14	Ordered	Bollinger/IncatUSA

Machinery: 4 x MTU 20V8000 M71L Diesels; 4 x Wartsila WLD 1400 SR Waterjets **Displacement:** 1,515 tons (light); 2,362 tons (FL) **Dimensions:** 103m x 28.5m x 3.83m **Speed:** Average 35 knots (43 knots without payload) **Range:** 1,200 miles (max transit); 5,600 miles (self-deployment) **Load:** 635 tons **Aircraft:** CH-53E capable flight deck **Complement:** 41

Notes: Originally known as the Joint High Speed Vessel program these vessels are a joint effort between the US Navy and the US Army that are suitable and useful for both branches. The original plan was to acquire ten ships with each branch having five vessels each, but this was subsequently changed to the MSC having overall control of the program to minimize duplication of effort and to save money.

Each Expeditionary Fast Transport ship's role is for the fast intra-theatre transportation of troops, military vehicles and equipment. They are capable of delivering 700 short tons 1,200 nautical miles at an average speed of 35 knots. The ships were designed to be able to operate within shallow draft ports and waterways and be able to transport the US Army's M1-A2 Abrams Main Battle Tank. Each ship is equipped with a large flight deck on the stern capable of operating the largest military helicopters in US Navy service. The design is adaptable with a reconfigurable 20,000 square foot mission bay area that can be quickly and relatively easily transformed to serve a number of different tasks from military hospital, carrying containerised cargo to support disaster relief operations.

In 2016 MILLINOCKET was fitted for trials of an electromagnetic railgun, but there are no plans to fit this on a permanent basis.

In 2015 Congress approved construction of an eleventh vessel of the class, with the twelfth approved in 2016. On 13 February 2018, Navy Secretary Richard V. Spencer announced the name of the latter as NEWPORT. The FY 2019 budget appropriations approved the construction of a thirteenth member of the class.

When originally announced as a separate Army and Navy programs, some of the vessels were to have had different names. CHOCKTAW COUNTY (ex VIGILANT); MILLINOCKET (ex FORTITUDE); TRENTON (ex RESOLUTE); BRUNSWICK (ex COURAGEOUS) and BISMARCK (ex SACRIFICE).

SPECIAL MISSION SHIPS

SEA BASED X-BAND RADAR

Ship	Hull Number	Completion Date	Builder
SBX-1	SBX-1	2005	Boeing/Vyborg

Displacement: 32,690 tons; 50,000 tons (Ballasted) **Dimensions:** 118.6m x 72.56m x 10m **Speed:** 9 knots **Complement:** 33 civilians + 49 military

Notes: Operated by the MSC since 2011 for the Missile Defense Agency, SBX-1 is a semi-submersible, self propelled platform that provides ballistic missile tracking information. She is part of America's ballistic missile defence system and was designed to be moored in Kuluk Bay, Alaska. The large radome that dominates the vessel was designed and built by American defence contractor Raytheon. The vessel was adapted from a Norwegian designed, Russian built, twin hulled semi-submersibile drilling rig. Conversion of the platform was carried out at Brownsville, Texas. For long distance voyages she is towed by tug or moved by heavy lift ship.

USNS Howard O. Lorenzen

MISSILE RANGE
INSTRUMENTATION SHIPS

Ship	Hull Number	Completion Date	Builder
HOWARD O. LORENZEN	T-AGM 25	2012	VT Halter Marine

Machinery: Diesel-Electric; each of four Main Diesel Generators is driven by a Cat/Mak 12M32C diesel engine; generator sets power two main motors connected in tandem to drive a single propeller; 1 Shaft **Displacement:** 12,575 tons **Dimensions:** 163m x 27m x 6.4m **Speed:** 20 knots **Complement:** 88 mixed mariners and civilians

Notes: VT Halter Marine, in 2006, was awarded the contract to construct a ship to carry the Cobra Judy radar and HOWARD O. LORENZEN was the resulting vessel. Her role is to collect ballistic missile data in support of international treaty verification using the advanced and classified Cobra Judy radar that was jointly developed by Northrop Grummand and Raytheon.

USNS Invincible

INVINCIBLE CLASS

Ship	Hull Number	Completion Date	Builder
INVINCIBLE	T-AGM 24	1986	Tacoma Boatbuilding

Machinery: Four diesel generators driving two shafts; 1,600 shp **Displacement:** 2,262 tonnes (FL) **Dimensions:** 68.3m x 13.1m x 4.5m **Speed:** 11 knots **Complement:** 18 Civilians; 18 Military

Notes: INVINCIBLE is a converted member of the Stalwart T-AGOS vessel and now provides a platform to take a dual band Cluster Gemini radar to sea on behalf of the US Air Force. The radar has been developed to collect information to support theatre ballistic missile requirements. INVINCIBLE operates primarily in the Indian Ocean and Arabian Sea monitoring the activities of North Korea and China.

USNS Henson

OCEANOGRAPHIC SURVEY SHIPS
PATHFINDER CLASS

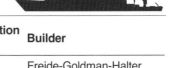

Ship	Hull Number	Completion Date	Builder
PATHFINDER	T-AGS 60	1994	Freide-Goldman-Halter
BOWDITCH	T-AGS 62	1996	Freide-Goldman-Halter
HENSON	T-AGS 63	1998	Freide-Goldman-Halter
BRUCE C. HEEZEN	T-AGS 64	2000	Freide-Goldman-Halter
MARY SEARS	T-AGS 65	2001	Freide-Goldman-Halter
MAURY	T-AGS 66	2015	VT Halter Marine

Machinery: Diesel-electric; 4 EMD/Baylor diesel generators; 2 GE CDF 1944 motors
Displacement: 4,762 tons (FL) **Dimensions:** 100.1m x 17.7m x 5.8m **Speed:** 16 knots
Complement: 25 plus 27 scientists

Notes: The first five vessels, plus a sixth SUMNER (decommissioned in 2014), were ordered in 1991 to provide oceanographic surveys across the world. In December 2009 an additional ship was ordered from VT Halter Marine. Each ship is equipped with three multi-purpose cranes and five winches together with world class oceanographic equipment including multi-beam echo sounders, towed sonars and expendable sensors. MAURY is slightly larger than her sister ships being 7 metres longer in order to accommodate a 5.5x 5.5 m moonpool for 'through hull' launch and recovery of scientific research equipment.

OCEANOGRAPHIC SURVEY SHIP

Ship	Hull Number	Completion Date	Builder
-----	T-AGS 67	Building	VT Halter Marine

Notes: In late 2018 the US Naval Sea System Command handed VT Halter Marine a US$9 million contract for the purchase of long lead items, limited advanced production and further design engineering for the future Oceanographic Survey ship (T-AGS 67). The design will be a follow on class to the T-AGS 60 class but based on USNS MAURY the last of the Pathfinder Class which commissioned into service in 2015. The T-AGS 67 will be equipped with a wide range of systems to allow the ships to collect a huge range of biological, acoustic and specific surveying. Each projected ship will be able to deploy a 34 foot hydrographic launch that can collect survey data in waters up to 4000 feet deep.

OCEANOGRAPHIC SURVEY SHIPS
NEIL ARMSTRONG CLASS

Ship	Hull Number	Completion Date	Builder
NEIL ARMSTRONG	AGOR 27	2015	Dakota Creek Industries
SALLY RIDE	AGOR 28	2016	Dakota Creek Industries

Machinery: 2 Siemens AC Electric Motors **Displacement:** 3,043 tons **Dimensions:** 73m x 15m x 4.57m **Speed:** 12 knots **Range:** 10,545 nautical miles **Complement:** 20 crew plus 24 scientists

Notes: This class of oceanographic survey ships are named after famous NASA astronauts with the first two ships named after the first man on the moon and the first American woman in space. These ships are owned by the US Navy but operated on their behalf by the Woods Hole Oceanographic Institution. AGOR 27 was ordered in May 2010 but sadly Neil Armstrong died before he could see the ship commissioned into service, a role performed by his second wife Carol. Sister ship SALLY RIDE is being operated by the Scripps Institution of Oceanography under a renewable charter party agreement. The design of the ships is a commercially available design capable of coastal and deep ocean surveys. Both ships have state-of-the-art equipment together with worldwide land-based communications.

USNS Waters

NAVIGATION TEST SUPPORT SHIP
WATERS CLASS

Ship	Hull Number	Completion Date	Builder
WATERS	T-AGS 45	1993	NG Avondale

Machinery: Diesel-electric, twin-screw; 7,400 shp **Displacement:** 12,403 tons (FL)
Dimensions: 139.3m x 21m x 6.4m **Speed:** 13 knots **Complement:** 32 civilians and 59 technicians

Notes: Originally delivered as an oceanographic survey ship in 1993 she was subsequently refitted in 1998 as a navigation test support ship. In this role she supports submarine navigation system testing and also provides ballistic missile flight test support services. Additionally WATERS has a centreline moonpool from which she can deploy recoverable ROVs.

US NAVY/MSC2 BRIAN G REYNOLDS   USNS Able

OCEAN SURVEILLANCE SHIPS
VICTORIOUS CLASS

Ship	Hull Number	Completion Date	Builder
VICTORIOUS	T-AGOS 19	1991	McDermott Inc
ABLE	T-AGOS 20	1991	McDermott Inc
EFFECTIVE	T-AGOS 21	1993	McDermott Inc
LOYAL	T-AGOS 22	1993	McDermott Inc

Machinery: Diesel-electric; 4 Caterpillar diesel generators, 2 GE motors, twin screw 1,600 shp; 2 bow thrusters **Displacement:** 3,396 tons (FL) **Dimensions:** 71.5m x 28.5m x 7.6m **Speed:** 16 knots **Complement:** 38

Notes: The Victorious-class ships are built on small waterplane twin hulls (SWATCH) which gives the ships greater levels of stability at slow speed in high latitudes under adverse weather conditions. The role of these ships is to gather underwater acoustical data. To achieve this they are fitted with a range of electronic equipment including a towed array system (SURTASS).

USNS Impeccable

IMPECCABLE CLASS

Ship	Hull Number	Completion Date	Builder
IMPECCABLE	T-AGOS 23	2001	Tamp SY/Halter Marine

Machinery: Diesel-electric; three diesel generators; 2 Westinghouse motors driving twin screw shaft; 2 omni-thruster hydrojets **Displacement:** 5,370 tonnes (FL) **Dimensions:** 85.8m x 29.2m x 7.9m **Speed:** 12 knots **Complement:** 26 Civilian; 19 Military

Notes: USNS IMPECCABLE is assigned to the Military Sealifts Commands Special Missions Program and conducts sensitive ocean surveillance roles on behalf of the US Government. Her keel was laid down on 2 February 1993 and her construction was completed in 2001. The delay in completion was due to difficulties experienced by the original shipyard and the 60 percent complete hull was completed at Halter Marine from 20 April 1995. The hull form is based on that used by the Victorious-class, but IMPEC-CABLE has a more powerful machinery arrangement designed for the use of active towed array systems. In March 2009 IMPECCABLE was at the centre of an incident involving a Chinese destroyer whilst operating in the South China Seas. The destroyer came within 100 yards of the surveillance vessel on numerous occasions, resulting in US President Barack Obama ordering the destroyer USS CHUNG HOON to assist.

CHARTERED SUPPORT VESSELS

Ship	Hull Number	Completion Date	Builder
HOS ARROWHEAD		2009	Leevac Shipyards
HOS BLACK POWDER		2009	Leevac Shipyards
HOS DOMINATOR		2002	Leevac Shipyards
HOS EAGLE VIEW		2009	Leevac Shipyards
HOS WESTWIND		2009	Leevac Shipyards
MV MALAMA		1981	Swiftships Inc
MV DOLORES CHOUEST		1978	North American SB
MV C-COMMANDO		1997	North American SB
MV C-CHAMPION		1997	North American SB

Machinery: Two Caterpillar 3516B diesels driving two shafts **Displacement:** 2,428 GT **Dimensions:** 76.2m x 16.46m x 4.52m **Speed:** 14 knots **Complement:** 11 (All figures for HOS Arrowhead)

Notes: MSC operates nine chartered vessels in support of the US Navy's submarine and special warfare requirements.

Vessels prefixed HOS have been chartered from Hornbeck Offshore. HOS WESTWOOD, HOS BLACK POWDER, HOS EAGLE VIEW and HOS ARROWHEAD provide escort support services for the US Navy's submarine force. HOS DOMINATOR provides submarine rescue support. She can carry the pressurised rescue module and atmosphere diving suits for submarine rescue and training operations.

MV MALAMA is a small 65 tons/110ft ferry boat providing an open ocean passenger transfer service to Pacific fleet submarines. The remaining vessels MV DOLORES CHOUEST, MV C-COMMANDO and MV C-CHAMPION support Naval Warfare Command requirements.

Military Sea Lift Command also operates two chemical tankers MT SLNC GOODWILL and MT SLNC PAX.

USNS Shughart

STRATEGIC SEALIFT SHIPS
LARGE, MEDIUM SPEED, RO-RO SHIPS

SHUGHART CLASS

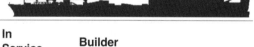

Ship	Hull Number	In Service	Builder
SHUGHART	T-AKR 295	1996	Odense Staal A/S Lindo Denmark
YANO	T-AKR 297	1997	Odense Staal A/S Lindo Denmark

Machinery: Two Burmeister & Wain diesels driving one shaft; 47,300 shp
Displacement: 55,123 tons **Dimensions:** 276.4m x 32.3m x 10.6m **Speed:** 24 knots
Complement: 45 (plus up to 100 USN/USMC)

Notes: Two ships taken up from trade from Maersk Line having first entered commercial service in 1981 and later lengthened in 1987 by Hyundai. In 1993 they were again converted at NASSCO in San Diego to serve as Strategic Sealift Ships. The refit saw the addition of a stern slewing ramp, side access hatches and improved cargo handling equipment. They are capable of handling containerised cargo and rolling stock between developed ports or via motorised barges at sea.

● MARITIME SEALIFT COMMAND **USNS Gordon (left) and USNS Gilliland**

GORDON CLASS

Ship	Hull Number	In Service	Builder
GORDON	T-AKR 296	1996	AS Burmeister & Wan Denmark
GILLILAND	T-AKR 298	1997	AS Burmeister & Wan Denmark

Machinery: Three Burmeister & Wain diesels driving three shafts; 1 x 31,400 shp; 2 x 23,600 shp **Displacement:** 57,000 tons **Dimensions:** 272.6m x 32.2m x 11m **Speed:** 24 knots **Complement:** 45 (+ 50 USN)

Notes: These massive ships have the capacity to carry an entire US Army Task Force, which comprises 58 tanks, 48 tracked vehicles, plus more than 900 trucks and other wheeled vehicles. A pair of 110 tons single pedestal twin cranes allow for ease of transfer of cargo to locations where dockside facilities are limited or non-existent.

USNS Seay

BOB HOPE CLASS

Ship	Hull Number	Completion Date	Builder
BOB HOPE	T-AKR 300	1998	NG Avondale
FISHER	T-AKR 301	1999	NG Avondale
SEAY	T-AKR 302	2000	NG Avondale
MENDONCA	T-AKR 303	2000	NG Avondale
PILILAAU	T-AKR 304	2001	NG Avondale
BRITTIN	T-AKR 305	2002	NG Avondale
BENAVIDEZ	T-AKR 306	2003	NG Avondale

Machinery: Four Colt Pielstick diesels driving two shafts; 65,160 shp **Displacement:** 62,096 tons **Dimensions:** 289.6m x 32.3m x 11.2m **Speed:** 24.9 knots **Complement:** 27 - accommodation for 95 (plus 300 troops)

Notes: Purpose built Large-Medium Speed Ro-Ro ships with a total cargo carrying capacity in excess of 380,000 square feet.

USNS Dahl

WATSON CLASS

Ship	Hull Number	Completion Date	Builder
WATSON	T-AKR 310	1998	NASSCO
SISLER	T-AKR 311	1998	NASSCO
DAHL	T-AKR 312	1999	NASSCO
RED CLOUD	T-AKR 313	2000	NASSCO
CHARLTON	T-AKR 314	2000	NASSCO
WATKINS	T-AKR 315	2001	NASSCO
POMEROY	T-AKR 316	2001	NASSCO
SODERMAN	T-AKR 317	2002	NASSCO

Machinery: Two GE LM2500-30 Gas Turbines driving two shafts; 64,000 shp **Displacement:** 62,700 tons **Dimensions:** 289.6m x 32.2m x 12.9m **Speed:** 24.9 knots **Complement:** 30

Notes: These eight ships are the largest gas turbine powered vessels in the world. Due to costs the original plans to have them achieve a speed of 36 knots was abandoned. Part of the Strategic Sealift Program, MSC's largest sealift ships preposition Army stocks and are also available to move common user cargoes.

USNS Sgt. Matej Kocak

CONTAINER/RO-RO SHIPS

SGT MATEJ KOCAK CLASS

Ship	Hull Number	In Service	Builder
SGT MATEJ KOCAK	T-AK 3005	1984	Sun SB, Chester PA
PFC EUGENE A. OBREGON	T-AK 3006	1985	Sun SB, Chester PA
MAJ STEPHEN W. PLESS	T-AK 3007	1985	Sun SB, Chester PA

Displacement: 19,588 tons **Dimensions:** 250.2m x 32.2m x 5.7m **Speed:** 23 knots
Complement: 85 (plus 7 MSC, 8 USN and 25 maintainers)

Notes: These ships which were delivered in the mid 1980s were subsequently enlarged by 157 feet amidships as well as a helicopter landing platform. Formerly based in the Mediterranean, each ship was intended to carry 25% of the vehicles, fuel and stores required to support a USMC Marine Expeditionary Brigade. These vessels were bought outright from Waterman Steamship Corp in 2009. The ships have twin 50 tons and 35 tons cranes forward of the bridge and a 30 tons travelling gantry crane.

USNS 1st Lt. Baldomero Lopez

2ND LT JOHN P. BOBO CLASS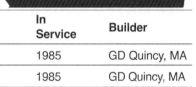

Ship	Hull Number	In Service	Builder
2nd LT JOHN P. BOBO	T-AK-3008	1985	GD Quincy, MA
PFC DEWAYNE T. WILLIAMS	T-AK 3009	1985	GD Quincy, MA
1st LT BALDOMERO LOPEZ	T-AK 3010	1985	GD Quincy, MA
1st LT JACK LUMMUS	T-AK 3011	1986	GD Quincy, MA
SGT WILLIAM R. BUTTON	T-AK 3012	1986	GD Quincy, MA

Machinery: Two Stork Werkspoor Diesels driving one shaft; 26,400 shp **Displacement:** 45,039 tons **Dimensions:** 205.9m x 32.2m x 9.8m **Speed:** 23 knots **Complement:** 38 civilians, 10 technicians.

Notes: These ships were built following the Reagan Administrations' plans to build up the strength and capabilities of the US Navy and Military Sealift Command. They were delivered from General Dynamics at Quincy in Massachusetts. They provide equipment to sustain a Marine Corps Air Ground Task Force for up to 30 days.

First ship is homeported in Europe with the remainder of the class based at Guam in the Pacific.

USNS Gunnery Sgt. Fred W. Stockham

GUNNERY SGT FRED W. STOCKHAM CLASS

Ship	Hull Number	In Service	Builder
GUNNERY SGT FRED W. STOCKHAM (ex-SODERMAN)	T-AK 3017	1997	Odense Staal A/S Lindo

Machinery: Two Burmeister & Wain diesels driving one shaft; 47,300 shp **Displacement:** 56,004 tons **Dimensions:** 276.6m x 32.3m x 10.6m **Speed:** 24 knots **Complement:** 26

Notes: Built in Denmark in 1980 as a conventional container ship, this vessel was acquired by the US Navy in the early 1990s. She was subsequently converted with the work being carried out by NASSCO at San Diego. She was commissioned into service in 1997 as USNS SODERMAN but in 2000 was transferred to the Maritime Pre-Positioning Force and her name was changed to GUNNERY SGT FRED W. STOCKHAM in 2001 so as not to cause any confusion with the Watson-class ship of the same name.

USNS 1st Lt. Harry L. Martin

1ST LT HARRY L. MARTIN CLASS

Ship	Hull Number	In Service	Builder
1st LT HARRY L. MARTIN	T-AK 3015	1980	Bremer Vulkan

Machinery: One Bremer Vulkan MAN diesel driving one shaft; 25,700 shp; bow and stern thrusters **Displacement:** 51,531 tons **Dimensions:** 230m x 32.3m x 10.9m **Speed:** 21.5 knots **Complement:** 27 civilians, 12 military technicians.

Notes: Built as a commercial container ship called TARAGO in Germany the ship was acquired by the United States in the mid 1990s for conversion into a Maritime Pre-Positioning Ship. The conversion work was undertaken by Atlantic Drydock in Jacksonville Florida and the ship, renamed as 1ST LT HARRY L. MARTIN was handed back in April 2000. Since then she has been based in European waters. She is currently classified as a dry cargo-carrying surge sealift asset.

USS Lance Cpl. Roy M. Wheat

LANCE CPL ROY M. WHEAT CLASS

Ship	Hull Number	In Service	Builder
LANCE CPL ROY M. WHEAT	T-AK 3016	2003	Chernomorskiy Zavod, Ukraine

Machinery: Two Mashproyect-Zorya M25 Gas Turbines driving two shafts; 18,000 shp each **Displacement:** 50,570 tons **Dimensions:** 263.1m x 30.01m x 10.67m **Speed:** 26.5 knots **Complement:** 25

Notes: This ship after acquisition has an 118 foot section inserted into her hull. She is government owned and is operated as a surge sealift vessel. She is reportedly very expensive to operate due to her former Eastern bloc heritage.

US NAVY/CMAS JOAN E. JENNINGS　　　　USNS Maj. Bernard F. Fisher

CONTAINER SHIPS
LTC CALVIN P. TITUS

Ship	Hull Number	In Service	Builder
MAJ BERNARD F. FISHER	T-AK 4396	1985	Odense Staal A/S Lindo

Machinery: 1 x Sulzer diesel driving one shaft; 23,030 shp **Displacement:** 48,000 tons **Dimensions:** 198.86m x 32.24m x 10.99m **Speed:** 19 knots **Complement:** 21.

Notes: Originally known as SEA FOX and renamed in October 1999; this vessel is named for US Air Force Medal of Honor recipient Bernard F. Fisher. She is owned and operated by Sealift, Inc of Oyster Bay, New York on behalf of the US Military Sealift Command and is assigned to Maritime Prepositioning Ship Squadron Three.

USNS SSGT Edward A. Carter

LTC JOHN U. D. PAGE

Ship	Hull Number	In Service	Builder
LTC JOHN U. D. PAGE	T-AK 4443	2001	Daewoo SB
SSGT EDWARD A. CARTER	T-AK 4544	2001	Daewoo SB

Machinery: 1 x Sulzer diesel driving one shaft; 13,800 shp **Displacement:** 81,284 tons **Dimensions:** 289.5m x 32.3m x 11.6m **Speed:** 18 knots **Complement:** 20 civilians.

Notes: These ships were first completed as container ships in 1985 with the names NEWARK BAY and OOCL INNOVATION. In 2001 they were acquired by the Military Sealift Command. Both are operated by Maersk Lines and are based in the Indian Ocean loaded with equipment required by the US Army. Each ship can carry 2,500 standard containers and provide 30 days sustainment for an Army Brigade Combat Team.

BUFFALO SOLDIER CLASS

Ship	Hull Number	In Service	Builder
TSGT JOHN A. CHAPMAN	T-AK 323	2002	Chantiers

Machinery: Pielstick medium speed diesel driving one shaft; 23,400 shp **Displacement:** 41,002 tons **Dimensions:** 204.2m x 26.5m x 10.5m **Speed:** 16 knots **Complement:** 19

Notes: This French built vessel was originally built for the Compagnie General Maritime as MV CGM UTRILLO. She was acquired in 1992 by American Automar, reflagged as an American ship and renamed as MC AMERCIAN MERLIN. On 8 April 2005 the ship was renamed to honour Pope Air Force Base combat controller Technical Sergeant John A. Chapman who had been awarded the Air Force Cross for his actions in the Battle of Takur Ghar. The ship is equipped with an all weather cocoon on the upperdeck. She is loaded with US Air Force munitions and other supplies. The ship is operated by Sealift Inc of Oyster Bay, New York.

USNS Lawrence H. Gianella

TRANSPORT TANKERS
CHAMPION CLASS

Ship	Hull Number	Completion Date	Builder
LAWRENCE H. GIANELLA	T-AOT 1125	1986	American SB

Machinery: One Mitsubishi or one Ishikawajima-Sulzer diesel driving one shaft; 15,300 shp **Displacement:** 39,000 tons approx **Dimensions:** 187.5m x 27.4m x 10.4m **Speed:** 16 knots **Complement:** 31

Notes: The sole survivor of a class built for long term charter to MSC. This ship is doubled hulled as well as strengthened for operations in ice and other extreme climates. She is primarily deployed on freighting duties.

When required she is able to rig replenishment gear. She was previously deployed at Diego Garcia as a strategic prepositioning ship but is now primarily used on freighting duties.

MV Maersk Peary

LONG TERM GOVERNMENT CHARTER

STATE CLASS

Ship	Hull Number	Completion Date	Builder
EMPIRE STATE	T-AOT 5193	2010	NASSCO
EVERGREEN STATE	T-AOT 5205	2011	NASSCO
MAERSK PEARY	T-AOT 5246	2004	STX Offshore

Machinery: One MAN Burmeister & Wain Alpha 6S50 MC diesel driving a single shaft; 2,665bhp **Displacement:** 57,818 tons approx **Dimensions:** 183m x 32.2m x 11.8m **Speed:** 14.8 knots **Complement:** 21

Notes: These vessels are used to transport refined petroleum products between refineries and military storage and distribution facilities, as they are doubled hulled. The ice-strengthened tanker MAERSK PEARY (T-AOT 5246) is on long-term charter to support bases in the Antarctic and Greenland.

MILITARY SEALIFT COMMAND   MV Mohegan

DRY CARGO SHIPS

Ship	Hull Number	Completion Date	Builder
MV BBC SEATTLE	T-AK 5272	1997	Flensburger Schiffsbau
MV MOHEGAN	T-AK 5158	1994	Orskov Christensens

Machinery: One MIT 6UEC50LSII diesel driving a single shaft **Displacement:** 20,406 tons approx **Dimensions:** 153m x 23.6m x 9.00m **Speed:** 15 knots **Complement:** 21(above details for BBC SEATTLE)

Notes: These two ships are under a long term charter with BBC SEATTLE providing dry cargo services worldwide. MV MOHEGAN meanwhile operates in the Indian Ocean between Singapore and Diego Garcia.

USNS Guam

HIGH SPEED VESSELS

Ship	Hull Number	Completion Date	Builder
GUAM	T-HST-1	2012	Austal USA

Machinery: Four Caterpillar 3618 Diesels; Four Rolls Roiyce KaMeWa Waterjets
Displacement: 1,646 tons **Dimensions:** 114m x 24m x 4.3m **Speed:** 35 knots **Decks:** 4
Capacity: 866 passengers and vehicles **Complement:** 21

Notes: In January 2010 the fast ferries HUAKAI and ALAKAI were used to assist in the Haiti earthquake relief effort having never entered commercial service. Seven months later the vessels were auctioned off for US$25 million a piece to the US Department of Transportation's Maritime Administration. In 2012 they were then transferred to the US Navy for use as troop transports. The two vessels, built in 2007 and 2008, were renamed GUAM and PUERTO RICO in May 2012. These vessels have 70 percent commonality with the T-EPFs in service with the US Navy. PUERTO RICO is currently on an Enhanced Use Lease in Nova Scotia.

USNS Montford Point

EXPEDITIONARY TRANSFER DOCK
MONTFORD POINT CLASS

Ship	Hull Number	In Service	Builder
MONTFORD POINT	T-ESD 1	2013	NASSCO
JOHN GLENN	T-ESD 2	2014	NASSCO

Machinery: Diesel Electric Propulsion; four MAN Burmeister & Wain medium speed main engines; 24Mw diesel electric plant; two shafts **Displacement:** 34,500 tons **Dimensions:** 239.3m x 50m x 9m **Speed:** 15 knots **Complement:** 34 MSC personnel

Notes: These ships are based on the hull form of the Alaska-class crude oil tanker, which NASSCO is famed for producing. The Mobile Landing Platform Ship is a semi-submersible ship designed to facilitate the loading and offloading of military equipment via LCAC. On deck there is space for 3 LCACs together with their support equipment. During build of the third vessel of the class, LEWIS B. PULLER, the ship was significantly altered to become a separate sub class.

USNS Lewis B. Puller

EXPEDITIONARY MOBILE BASE
LEWIS B. PULLER CLASS

Ship	Hull Number	Completion Date	Builder
LEWIS B. PULLER	T-ESB 3	2017	NASSCO
HERSCHEL 'WOODY' WILLIAMS	T-ESB 4	2018	NASSCO
MIGUEL KEITH	T-ESB 5	Building	NASSCO
----	T-ESB 6	Building	NASSCO

Machinery: Diesel Electric Propulsion; four MAN Burmeister & Wain medium speed main engines; 24Mw diesel electric plant; two shafts **Displacement:** 34,500 tons **Dimensions:** 233m x 50m x 7.8m **Speed:** 15 knots **Armament:** 12 x .50 calibre machine guns **Aircraft:** Up to 4 CH-53 heavy lift helicopters **Complement:** 5 officers, 96 enlisted and 44 merchant mariners

Notes: Originally ordered as sister ships to MONTFORD POINT and JOHN GLENN but subsequently altered during build to better reflect the need for Expeditionary Mobile Bases the ships differ significantly from the earlier vessels. Unlike the previous two ships these vessels are not semi-submersible and use cranes to lower boats weighing up to 11 tons into the water. They can be prepositioned off the target area with a large military force on board for low intensity missions. In so doing they will relieve the high value amphibious ships of the US Navy to more pressing and necessary tasks. They have been fitted with hangers for the embarked heavy lift helicopters. A sixth member of the class was ordered in October 2018.

USNS Curtiss

AVIATION LOGISTICS SHIPS

Ship	Hull Number	In Service	Builder
WRIGHT	T-AVB 3	1986	Ingalls SB
CURTISS	T-AVB 4	1987	Ingalls SB

Machinery: Two GE geared steam turbines driving one shaft; 30,000 shp **Displacement:** 12,409 tons **Dimensions:** 183.5m x 27.43m x 10.36m **Speed:** 23 knots **Complement:** 33 (plus 300 USMC)

Notes: These two ships' main role is to support the operation of the US Marine Corps helicopters. Whilst aviation facilities are limited to a helicopter flight deck forward of the derricks, the ships can accommodate a large amount deck of containers containing spares and other essential items. Vehicles can be offloaded by a stern ramp or side door. Both ships have ten 30 tons cranes and a single 70 tons crane for cargo handling. CURTISS and WRIGHT are both operated under contract by Crowley Liner Services and are part of the Ready Reserve Force but are dedicated to USMC Aviation Logistic Support.

US ARMY/MARICRIS C. MCLANE

MV VAdm. K. R. Wheeler

OFFSHORE PETROLEUM
DISTRIBUTION SHIP

Ship	Hull Number	In Service	Builder
VADM K. R. WHEELER	T-AG 5001	2007	Edison Chouest Offshore

Machinery: Two MAK V12 Diesels; 2 shafts; 16,314 hp **Displacement:** 10,404 tons
Dimensions: 106.22m x 21.33m x 6.9m **Speed:** 15 knots **Complement:** 22 civilians
(plus 8 USN)

Notes: This vessel is employed as an offshore pumping station for petroleum products required by American and Allied forces and is capable of pumping 500,000 barrels of oil products from up to eight miles offshore. The ship provides an important role when onshore facilities are inadequate or non existent. When on deployment she is assisted by the 165ft tender USNS FAST TEMPO and two amphibious vehicles.

The 1963 built SS PETERSBURG (T-AOT 9101), the former OPDS vessel, remains a part of the Ready Reserve Force and is laid up at Alameda in San Francisco Bay.

USNS Pollux

READY RESERVE FORCE
FAST SEALIFT SHIPS

Ship	Hull Number	In Service	Builder
ALGOL	T-AKR 287	1984	Rotterdamse DDM
BELLATRIX	T-AKR 288	1984	Rheinstaht NSW Emden
DENEBOLA	T-AKR 289	1985	Rotterdamse DDM
POLLUX	T-AKR 290	1986	AG Weser Bremen
ALTAIR	T-AKR 291	1985	Rheinstaht NSW Emden
REGULUS	T-AKR 292	1985	AG Weser Bremen
CAPELLA	T-AKR 293	1984	Rotterdamse DMM
ANTARES	T-AKR 294	1984	AG Weser Bremen

Machinery: Two GE MST19 geared steam turbines driving two shafts; 120,000 shp **Displacement:** 55,355 tons (FL) **Dimensions:** 288.4m x 32.3m x 10.8m **Speed:** 33 knots **Complement:** 42

Notes: These exceptionally fast ships can sail at speeds of up to 33 knots which allows them to sail from the US East Coast to Europe in just six days and to the Persian Gulf via the Suez Canal in just 18. Combined, all eight ships, can supply a full army mechanised division with all the supplies it needs. In 2008 all eight ships were transferred to the Ready Reserve Force and are stored in Reduced Operating Status (5) meaning they can be reactivated within five days when necessary.

ROLL ON/ROLL OFF SHIPS
ADMIRAL WM. M.
CALLAGHAN CLASS

Ship	Hull Number	In Service	Builder
GTS ADM Wm M. CALLAGHAN	T-AKR 1001	1967	Sun SB & DD Co

Machinery: Two GE LM2500 Gas Turbines; two shafts; 40,000 shp **Displacement:** 13,161 tons (light); 26,537 tons (FL) **Dimensions:** 211.6m x 28m x 5.18m **Speed:** 26 knots **Complement:** 28 (when operational), 9 when in reserve

Notes: This vessel was the first US Navy vessel to be fitted with gas turbine propulsion as well as being the first roll on/roll off vessel for the Navy. The current General Electric LM2500 gas turbines were fitted in the ship in 1997. The ship has a capacity to carry up to 750 vehicles and 212 standard containers. She is equipped with a variety of cranes to aid the offloading of the vehicles and supplies. Her prefix of GTS stands for Gas Turbine Ship. She is currently berthed in Alameda in California where she is in Reduced Operational Status (5) which means she can be returned to operational service within five days.

CAPE D CLASS

Ship	Hull Number	To RRF	Builder
CAPE DUCATO	T-AKR 5051	1985	Chantiers
CAPE DOUGLAS	T-AKR 5052	1985	Eriksberg
CAPE DOMINGO	T-AKR 5053	1985	Chantiers
CAPE DECISION	T-AKR 5054	1985	Eriksberg
CAPE DIAMOND	T-AKR 5055	1985	Chantiers

Machinery: Chantiers built - Three Pielstick diesels; One Shaft; 28,890 shp; Eriksberg built - Three Lindholmen diesels; One shaft; 27,000 shp **Displacement:** 13,140 tons (Light); 34,790 tons (FL) **Dimensions:** 207.4m x 29.6m x 4.11m **Speed:** 16 knots **Complement:** 27

Notes: Container-RoRo vessels are all based at Charleston, South Carolina at Reduced Operational Station (ROS) (5).

CAPE E CLASS

Ship	Hull Number	To RRF	Builder
CAPE EDMONT	T-AKR 5069	1987	Eriksberg

Machinery: Three Pielstick diesels; one shaft; 25,920 shp **Displacement:** 12,256 tons (light); 32,543 tons (FL) **Dimensions:** 199.1m x 28.7m x 3.8m **Speed:** 16 knots **Complement:** 27

Notes: A combination container-RoRo ship she is based at Charleston, South Carolina at ROS (5).

CAPE H CLASS

Ship	Hull Number	To RRF	Builder
CAPE HUDSON	T-AKR 5066	1986	Tangan Vaerft
CAPE HENRY	T-AKR 5067	1986	Mitsubishi Heavy Ind
CAPE HORN	T-AKR 5068	1986	Kaldnes Mek Versted

Machinery: One Burmeister & Wain (CAPE HENRY: Mitsubishi-Sulzer) diesel; one shaft; 30,700 shp (CAPE HENRY: 30,150 shp) **Displacement:** 19,091 tons (light); 51,007 tons (FL) **Dimensions:** 228.5m x 32.3m x 4.7m **Speed:** 18 knots **Complement:** 28

Notes: All three ships differ slightly from one another. Each ship includes a 34,000 square foot hoistable deck. There are four internal vehicle decks and there is space enough to carry around 1600 standard 20ft containers. All ships are now based at San Francisco.

CAPE I CLASS

Ship	Hull Number	To RRF	Builder
CAPE ISLAND	T-AKR 10	1993	Bath Iron Works
CAPE INTREPID	T-AKR 11	1986	Bath Iron Works
CAPE ISABEL	T-AKR 5062	1986	Bath Iron Works
CAPE INSCRIPTION	T-AKR 5076	1987	Bath Iron Works

Machinery: Two sets GE Geared Turbines; two shafts, 37,000 shp **Displacement:** 14,767 tons (light); 33,900 tons (FL) **Dimensions:** 208.7m x 31m x 5.2m **Speed:** 18 knots **Complement:** 31

Notes: Ro-Ro vehicle carriers with stern ramp and sideports for the rapid loading and unloading of vehicles. All are at ROS (5) with CAPE ISLAND and CAPE INTREPID based at Tacoma in Washington State with the other pair at Long Beach in California.

CAPE K CLASS

Ship	Hull Number	To RRF	Builder
CAPE KNOX	T-AKR 5082	1995	Nippon Kokan
CAPE KENNEDY	T-AKR 5083	1995	Nippon Kokan

Machinery: One Sumitomo-Sulzer diesel; one shaft; 25,400 shp **Displacement:** 36,450 tons (FL) **Dimensions:** 212.1m x 32.3m x 10.72m **Speed:** 17.6 knots **Complement:** 25

Notes: These ships have two vehicle decks and can also be used to transport 1,550 standard 20ft containers. Both are based at New Orleans, Louisiana at ROS (5).

CAPE O CLASS

Ship	Hull Number	To RRF	Builder
CAPE ORLANDO	T-AKR 2044	1994	Kokums AB Malmo
nt	12,500		tons

Machinery: Two Cegielski-Sulzer diesels; One shaft; 21,600 shp **Displacement:** 12,500 tons (light); 32,799 tons (FL) **Dimensions:** 193.63m x 28.01m x 3.94m **Speed:** 22 knots **Complement:** 30

Notes: First built for Finnlines in 1981 as MV FINNEAGLE. She is now a vehicle RoRo vessel with stern ramps and 166,670 square feet of vehicle space. She can also carry 1,040 containers. At ROS (5) she is based at Alameda, California.

CAPE R CLASS

Ship	Hull Number	To RRF	Builder
CAPE RACE	T-AKR 9960	1994	Kawasaki Heavy Ind
CAPE RAY	T-AKR 9679	1994	Kawasaki Heavy Ind
CAPE RISE	T-AKR 9678	1994	Kawasaki Heavy Ind

Machinery: Two Kawasaki-MAN diesels; one shaft; 28,000 shp **Displacement:** 32,000 tons (FL) **Dimensions:** 197.52m x 32.26m x 8.5m **Speed:** 17.6 knots **Complement:** 29 (Full Operating Status); 9 (Reserve)

Notes: These three ships were originally built for Saudi Arabia but were later acquired to provide extra capacity. They operate as combination vehicle and container ships (1,315 standard containers). All are based at Portsmouth, Virginia.

CAPE T CLASS

Ship	Pennant Number	To RRF	Builder
CAPE TAYLOR	T-AKR 113	1994	Sasebo Heavy Ind
CAPE TEXAS	T-AKR 112	1994	HDW Kiel
CAPE TRINITY	T-AKR 9711	1994	HDW Kiel

Machinery: Two MAN diesels; one shaft; 18,980 shp **Displacement:** 9,870 tons (light); 24,551 tons (FL) **Dimensions:** 191.29m x 27.21m x 4.05m **Speed:** 20.5 knots **Complement:** 27 (Full Operating Status); 9 (Reserve)

Notes: Large container RoRo ships which have been equipped with ice strengthened hulls to allow them to operate in extreme weather conditions. All are based at Houston, Texas and are in ROS (5).

CAPE V CLASS

Ship	Hull Number	To RRF	Builder
CAPE VICTORY	T-AKR 9701	1993	Fincantieri, Genoa
CAPE VINCENT	T-AKR 9666	1993	Fincantieri, Genoa

Machinery: One GMT-Sulzer diesel; one shaft; 11,850 shp **Displacement:** 27,000 tons (FL) **Dimensions:** 192m x 26.55m x 8.47m **Speed:** 16 knots **Complement:** 25

Notes: Combination container/RoRo vehicle carrier. Spar decks added in 1998 to provide additional vehicle capacity. Based at Beaumont, Texas at ROS (5).

CAPE W CLASS

Ship	Hull Number	To RRF	Builder
CAPE WASHINGTON	T-AKR 9961	1994	Stocznia, Poland
CAPE WRATH	T-AKR 9962	1994	Stocznia, Poland

Machinery: One Cegielski-Sulzer diesel; one shaft; 17,400 shp **Displacement:** 47,000 tons (FL) **Dimensions:** 212.6m x 32.28m x 11.63m **Speed:** 17 knots **Complement:** 28

Notes: These former car carriers have received stronger decks in order to carry heavy military vehicles and tanks. They are based at Baltimore, Maryland in ROS (5).

MV Cape Mohican

SEABEE SHIP

Ship	Hull Number	To RRF	Builder
CAPE MAY	T-AKR 5063	1986	GD Quincy
CAPE MOHICAN	T-AKR 5065	1986	GD Quincy

Machinery: Two sets GE Geared Steam Turbines; one shaft; 36,000 shp **Displacement:** 18,880 tons (light) **Dimensions:** 266.4m x 32.3m x 5.4m **Speed:** 20.5 knots **Complement:** 34

Notes: These two ships have three decks on which cargo barges or container flats are stowed. A special Transporter (conveyor) system aboard the ships allow barges to be brought onto the ship via a stern elevator and transported around the ship by the same system. A total of 38 barges can be carried. CAPE MAY is laid up at Norfolk, Virginia and the other is at Alameda in California at ROS (5).

MV Gem State

AUXILIARY CRANE SHIPS
KEYSTONE STATE CLASS

Ship	Hull Number	To RRF	Builder
KEYSTONE STATE	T-ACS 1	1984	NASSCO
GEM STATE	T-ACS 2	1985	NASSCO
GRAND CANYON STATE	T-ACS 3	1987	NASSCO

Machinery: Two sets GE Geared Steam Turbines; one shaft; 19,250 shp
Displacement: 16,599 tons (light); 31,500 tons (FL) **Dimensions:** 203.8m x 23.2m x 5.8m **Speed:** 18 knots **Complement:** 64

Notes: Originally built as container ships and subsequently converted with the addition of three twin boom 30 tons pedestal cranes in order to lift containers and other cargo from themselves or other adjacent ships. The four forward cranes can be ganged together to lift 150 tons. All are based at Alameda in California.

MV Gopher State

GOPHER STATE CLASS

Ship	Hull Number	To RRF	Builder
GOPHER STATE	T-ACS 4	1988	Bath Iron Works
FLICKERTAIL STATE	T-ACS 5	1988	Bath Iron Works
CORNHUSKER STATE	T-ACS 6	1988	Bath Iron Works

Machinery: Two sets GE Geared Steam Turbines; one shaft; 17,500 shp **Displacement:** 15,060 tons (light); 26,670 tons (FL) **Dimensions:** 205.7m x 24.4m x 10.3m **Speed:** 20 knots **Complement:** 52

Notes: Former container ships converted at Norfolk Shipbuilding and Dry Dock in Virginia. All are based at Newport News.

USNS Pokagon

NATICK CLASS HARBOUR TUGS

Ship	Hull Number	Completion Date	Builder
CANONCHET	YTB 823	1973	Marinette Marine
DEKANWIDA	YTB 831	1974	Marinette Marine
KEOKUK	YTB 771	1964	Mobile Ship Repair
POKAGON	YTB 836	1975	Marinette Marine
SANTAQUIN	YTB 824	1973	Marinette Marine
SKENANDOA	YTB 835	1975	Marinette Marine
WANAMASSA	YTB 820	1973	Marinette Marine

Machinery: 1 Fairbanks-Morse 3808 1/8 diesel; 2000hp; one shaft **Displacement:** 362 tons (FL) **Dimensions:** 33m x 9.4m x 4.3m **Speed:** 12 knots **Complement:** 12

Notes: These are the last surviving members of the Natick-class of harbour tugs. These tugs can trace their lineage back to the 1960s when 77 of the class were operational around the United States. These eight tugs will in due course be replaced by new construction. All are named for Native American peoples. YTB 771 is located at NSA Portsmouth, New Hampshire; YTB 820, 824 and 831 are at NS Guantanamo Bay in Cuba. YTB 823 and 835 are at Kipsap. YTB 836 is located at NS Everett in Washington State.The class is being withdrawn from service and replaced by Military Sealift charters or YT-802 class vessels.

CONVERTED ASD HARBOUR TUGS

Ship	Hull Number	Completion Date	Builder
MANHATTAN	YT 800	1965	Marinette Marine
WASHTUNCA	YT 801	1973	Marinette Marine

Machinery: 2 Caterpillar 3516 diesels; 4000hp; Azimuthing Stern Drive
Displacement: 362 tons (FL) **Dimensions:** 33m x 9.4m x 4.3m **Speed:** 12 knots
Complement: 12

Notes: Originally members of the Nanick Class (YTB 779 and YTB 826) but these two vessels were converted in the mid-2000s with the addition of azimuthing stern drive propulsion units. They were returned to the US Navy in 2006 with both in service at NB Kitsap.

LONG TERM GOVERNMENT CHARTER
MAERSK PERRY CLASS

Ship	Pennant Number	Completion Date	Builder
MAERSK PERRY	T-AOT 5246	2004	STX Offshore Marine & Shipbuilding, South Korea

Machinery: Hyundai MAN and B&W 7S50MC-C diesel driving one shaft; 15,000 shp
Displacement: 38,177 tons (FL) **Dimensions:** 180m x 32m x 10.275m **Speed:** 14.8 knots **Complement:** 21

Notes: This vessel was originally built in 2004 for a Norwegian concern and named MT JUTUL. Seven years later in 2011 Maersk secured the long term contract to supply American military facilities at Thule Air Force Base in Greenland and McMurdo Station in Antarctica. The ship was repainted blue and reflagged as an American ship and leased to the Military Sealift Command.

APL 35 CLASS BARRACKS SHIPS

Ship	Hull Number	Completion Date	Builder
ASTOR	APL 18	1944	Tampa Shipbuilding

Machinery: 3 Diesel drive 100Kw 450 AC generators for electricity **Displacement:** 2,660 tons (FL) **Dimensions:** 79.1m x 14.63m x 3.04m **Accommodation:** 655 personnel

Notes: Originally built during World War Two and still in use today this vessel is likely one of the first to be replaced by a new series of barrack ships ordered in late 2018. APL 18 is currently in use as part of the CincPacFlt Berthing and Messing Program and is located at San Diego.

APL 35 CLASS BARRACKS SHIPS

Ship	Hull Number	Completion Date	Builder
MERCER	APL 39	1945	Boston Navy Yard
NUECES	APL 40	1945	Boston Navy Yard

Displacement: 4,080 tons **Dimensions:** 100m x 15m x 3.4m **Accommodation:** 1,226 personnel

Notes: APL 39 is the former USS MERCER built on the hull of an LST and started her career at New York on 7 November 1945. APL40 is the former USS NUECES. Both vessels served as barrack ships in the Vietnam War. On 7 March 2001 APL 39 was reclassified as Barracks Ship (non self propelled) and is currently in use at Sasebo in Japan. APL 40 is in a similar role at Yokosuka, Japan.

APL 39 and APL40 are likely to the first barrack ships to be replaced by new build vessels ordered in late 2018.

JOHN LEWIS CLASS OILER

Ship	Pennant Number	Completion Date	Builder
JOHN LEWIS	T-AO 205	2020	GD NASSCO
HARVEY MILK	T-AO 206	2021	GD NASSCO
EARL WARREN	T-AO 207	2022	GD NASSCO
ROBERT F. KENNEDY	T-AO 208	2023	GD NASSCO
LUCY STONE	T-AO 209	2024	GD NASSCO
SOJOURNER TURNER	T-AO 210	2035	GD NASSCO
Unnamed	T-AO 211	---	GD NASSCO
Unnamed	T-AO 212	---	GD NASSCO
Unnamed	T-AO 213	---	GD NASSCO
Unnamed	T-AO 214	---	GD NASSCO
Unnamed	T-AO 215	---	GD NASSCO
Unnamed	T-AO 216	---	GD NASSCO
Unnamed	T-AO 217	---	GD NASSCO
Unnamed	T-AO 218	---	GD NASSCO
Unnamed	T-AO 219	---	GD NASSCO
Unnamed	T-AO 220	---	GD NASSCO
Unnamed	T-AO 221	---	GD NASSCO

Machinery: 2 diesel engines producing 35,000sh **Displacement:** 43,000 tons (FL) **Dimensions:** About 675 feet x 100 feet x 35 feet x 9.4m x 4.3m **Speed:** 20 knots **Aircraft:** Helicopter platform and refuelling capability **Complement:** 75 civilian + 20 USN

Notes: This class has been designed as the eventual replacement vessels for the long serving Henry J. Kaiser-class oilers. As part of the Trump administration's plans to expand the US Navy fleet there will be seventeen John Lewis oilers in place of the fifteen older vessels. The first steel plates of USNS JOHN LEWIS were laid down at the San Diego shipyard of General Dynamics NASSCO in September 2018 with an expected completion date sometime in 2020. The first six vessels of the class were ordered as a batch order with the other five vessels completing by 2023. The John Lewis Class will be able to carry the equivalent of 156,000 barrels of fuel oil as well as a significant capacity of dry cargo and aviation refuelling capability. All seventeen ships will bear the names of human or civil rights activists.

NATIONAL DEFENCE RESERVE FLEET

Several ships remain in the custody of the Maritime Administration (MARAD). These ships range in role and are placed strategically around the United States in either the Retention or Non Retention categories. MARAD vessels are being preserved for federal agency programs. These ships are further categorised as follows:

RETENTION

ES	Emergency Sealift	Vessel reserved for sealift support for emergent requirements
FS	Fleet Support	Vessel reserved for Reserve Fleet organization use (eg, for material storage purposes)
IH	Interim Hold	Vessel being preserved pending future determination of status
LS	Logistics Support	Vessel reserved for cannibalisation or material stripping to support one or more RRF vessels
MU	Militarily Useful	Vessel reserved for future military or strategic use as determined by DoD program sponsors
NR	National Register	Vessel listed on the National Register and being preserved pending future donation or mitigation
SS	School Ship	Vessel on loan as a Training Ship to a US Maritime Academy
OAU	Other Agency Use	Vessel being operated by MARAD in support of other federal agency programs or missions
TU	Training Use	Vessel reserved as a training platform for one or more federal agencies

Ship	Hull No.	Status	Location
CAPE ANN	AK 5009	TU	James River, Virginia
CAPE BOVER	AK 5057	LS	Suisun Bay, California
CAPE CHALMERS	AK-5036	TU	Charleston, South Carolina
CAPE GIRARDEAU	AK 2039	LS	Suisun Bay, California
CAPE JACOB	T-AK 5029	LS	Suisun Bay, California
CAPE JUBY	T-AK 5077	LS	James River, Virginia
CAPE NOME	AK 1014	LS	James River, Virginia
CAPE FAREWELL	AK 5073	MU	Beaumont, Texas
CAPE FEAR	AK 5061	LS	Suisun Bay, California
CAPE FLATTERY	AK 5070	MU	Beaumont, Texas
CAPE MENDOCINO	AKR 5064	LS	Beaumont, Texas
PAUL BUCK	T-AOT 1122	IH	Beaumont, Texas
RICHARD G. MATHIESEN	T-AOT 1124	MU	Beaumont, Texas

Ship	Hull No.	Status	Location
SAMUEL L. COBB	T-AOT1123	IH	Beaumont, Texas
DIAMOND STATE	T-ACS 7	LS	Beaumont, Texas
GREEN MOUNTAIN STATE	T-ACS 9	LS	Suisun Bay, California
DEL MONTE	MA 200	TU	Little Creek, Virginia
SAVANNAH	55	NR	Baltimore, MD
EMPIRE STATE	TAP 1001	SS	Ft Schuyler, NY
GOLDEN BEAR	T-AGS 39	SS	Vallejo, California
KENNEDY	T-AK 5059	SS	Buzzards Bay, MA
STATE OF MAINE	T-AGS 40	SS	Castine. ME
GENERAL RUDDER	T-AGOS 2	SS	Galveston, Texas
STATE OF MICHIGAN	T-AGOS 6	SS	Traverse City, MI
TRIUMPH	T-AGOS 4	LS	Suisun Bay, California

NON-RETENTION

MARAD vessels that no longer have a useful application and are pending disposition.

DH Donation Hold — Vessel reserved for donation to a qualified memorial or non-profit humanitarian organization

HR Historic Review — Vessel awaiting review for National Register eligibility

S Stripping — Vessel in the process of being stripped of useful material prior to becoming available for disposal

D Disposal — Vessel available for disposal or in the process of being disposed

SAR Sold Awaiting Removal — Vessel sold and awaiting removal from the fleet site

Ship	Hull No.	Status	Location
CHESAPEAKE	AOT 5084	S	Beaumont, Texas
CAPE LOBOS	AKR 5078	D	Beaumont, Texas
HARKNESS	T-AGS 32	D	Brownsville, Texas
OBSERVATION ISLAND	T-AGM 28	D	Beaumont, Texas
SIMON LAKE	AS-33	D	James River, Virginia
SUMNER	T-AGS 61	D	Beaumont, Texas
TRIPOLI	LPH-10	D	Beaumont, Texas
EQUALITY STATE	T-ACS	D	Beaumont, Texas
CAPE ALAVA	AK 5012	D	James River, Virginia

Ship	Hull No.	Status	Location
CAPE ALEXANDER	AK 5010	D	James River, Virginia
CAPE ARCHWAY	AK 5011	D	James River, Virginia
CAPE AVINOFF	AK 5013	S	James River, Virginia
CAPE BORDA	AK 5058	D	Brownsville, Texas
CAPE BRETON	AK 5056	D	Brownsville, Texas
CAPE GIBSON	AK 5051	D	Beaumont, Texas
CAPE JOHNSON	T-AK 5075	D	Brownsville, Texas
CAPE FLORIDA	AK 5071	S	Beaumont, Texas

VESSELS HELD UNDER CUSTODY

Ship	Hull No.	Status	Location
BRAVANTE IX	SV 290	-	Beaumont, Texas
IRIS	WLB 395	-	Suisun Bay, California
PLANETREE	WLB 307	-	Suisun Bay, California
NASSAU	LHA 4	-	Beaumont, Texas

USN & USMC AVIATION

Second only in scale and operational capability to the United States Air Force, the USN and USMC is one of the world's pre-eminent air forces. That it retains such a powerful fighting force is through persistence and playing the political game against the USAF which wanted to control all aviation assets whereever they might be deployed, even at sea. Today the United States Navy owns and operates every single type of aircraft with the exception of heavy large strategic bombers and all are of equal quality and sophistication to the USAF fleet.

Uniquely the USN and USMC deploy both fixed wing and rotary wing aviation assets, whereas the US Air Force has shied away from owning large numbers of helicopters and the US Army has virtually no aircraft of its own at all. The US Navy organises its aircraft essentially between land based operations and those from naval vessels at sea.

At the heart of American naval policy is the aircraft carrier and the F-18 Hornet is by far the most numerous aircraft available to military commanders today. The F-18 started life back in the late 1970s as the YF-17 prototype which has subsequently been refined and modified and has remained in near constant production since the early 1980s. Today's latest iteration of the design is the F/A-18E/F/G Super Hornet and Growler, which is over 25 percent larger than the original A/B/C and D variants of the Hornet. Increasingly the Hornet will be acting alongside the F-35 Lightning II. The US Navy will operate the C variant that is capable of aircraft carrier take-off and landings and has somewhat longer range than its stable mate the F-35B vertical take-off and landing variant which the US Marine Corps will progressively introduce into service and replace their somewhat elderly Harrier Jump Jets in service. The F-35 is a fifth generation warplane with superb stealth technologies. The Navy, had originally seen the Lightning as a long term replacement for the Hornet and Super Hornet but under current plans they will not acquire nearly enough aircraft to fully replace the Hornet in service.

The US Navy aircraft carriers operate a range of aircraft in support roles including the E-2 Hawkeye aerial surveillance and battle management aircraft easily identifiable by the large radome placed on the back of its fuselage. Like the Hornet the Hawkeye is an elderly design kept current by retrofitting new technologies and software into the aircraft. The C-2 Greyhound is the Carrier on Board delivery aircraft that can bring urgently needed equipment and personnel to the aircraft carriers. The Greyhound is old and is progressively being replaced by a new variant of the MV-22 Osprey, which has been adapted so that it can carry a single engine for the F-35 Lightning. Aircraft carriers also operate a number of helicopters in support roles and for anti-submarine detection and destruction.

US Navy aviation is not limited to aircraft carriers with all major assets deploying with a single or twin helicopters for anti-submarine, anti-ship and general duties as well as land based operations around the globe. In the last ten years the role of aerial reconnaissance and surveillance has started to be taken over by the P-8A Poseidon long range aircraft. These assets are progressively replacing the Lockheed P-3 Orions in service but only relatively slowly and the Orion will still be in use for some time to come.

Of greater interest to many in the US Navy is the role that drones will play in the future. Already in use from larger naval vessels drones such as the Fire Scout, MQ-4C Triton and MQ-25A Stingray will in years to come take on many of the roles currently utilising manned aircraft and take the human out of harms way. In late 2018 the US Navy announced that it had placed a US$805 million fixed price contract for the design, development, fabrication, test, delivery and support of four MQ-25A unmanned air vehicles. Whilst the days of manned flight are far from over robots will increasingly take their place alongside conventional aircraft in the US Navy battle plan.

The US Marine Corps operates alongside their Navy cousins with a similar array of aviation assets. The MV-22C Osprey is perhaps the most important aircraft in their inventory after the FA-18 Super Hornets. The Osprey, after a torturous development phase, has now become a mainstay of the Corps operating plan. Able to deliver large numbers of men and equipment quicker and over longer distances than conventional helicopters, the Osprey is battle proven. It has also started to replace helicopters in the role of Marine One, the US President's Marine transportation. The F-35B is also making its presence felt as it gradually replaces the legacy Harrier jump jets.

US MARINE CORPS ROTARY AVIATION 2018-2030

The US Marine Corps is without doubt one of the world's most powerful fighting forces. Its inventory aircraft is amongst the best equipped on the planet but maintaining and enhancing its efficiency and potential are an ongoing struggle. With the election of President Donald Trump the USMC have a President willing to expand the US Military and such a direction could not have come at a better time for the service with many aircraft having seen fifteen years of arduous service in warzones around the world.

Today the USMC's core rotary assets comprise the Bell AH-1W/Z attack and UH-1Y utility aircraft, the heavy lift CH-53E Super Stallion, the Bell Boeing MV-22 Osprey tilt rotor and the Sikorsky VH-3D Sea Kings and UH-60N Black Hawk Presidential transport.

Currently, the USMC's largest ongoing project is focused on the replacement of the Lockheed Martin CH-53E with the CH-53K King Stallion. The new aircraft, whilst similar in appearance and physical size, is a huge leap forward in performance, payload capacity and range. The program will see the first CH-53K's in service by December 2019. The current E variants are spread between full squadrons of 16 aircraft with further subdivision of 12, 8 and 4. Only fully equipped squadrons are capable of performing a full range of requirements. The reason for this arrangement is because the USMC is 45 aircraft short of its needs with 145 operational. When the K variants enter service it is expected that together with modernized Es the full squadron system will be fully restored. Eight full squadrons, two reserve units each with eight helicopters will be supported by a single Fleet Replacement Squadron with 21 machines available. The current order book of 200 aircraft is still, however, some 20 aircraft short of the stated aims of the USMC.

The first CH-53K arrived at Marine Air Station New River in May 2018 for tests and evaluation. The IOC is expected for December 2019. The build up to full Operational Capability will see the 1st and 3rd Marine Air Wings established in GY2026, 2027 and 2029 respectively.

Legacy Sea Stallion aircraft are expected to be withdrawn around 2022. The E model will continue in service with the Marine Corps until around FY2032. The Es will, in order to get to this out of service date, be equipped with new avionics including the Smart Multifunction Colour Display (SMFCD) kits, the installation of SRD with Link 16 and embedded Satcom.

Power will come from the latest General Electric T-64-GE-419 engines. The Es will also receive BAE Systems ALE-47 countermeasures dispensing system and the AAR-47 multi spectral Threat warning system. In all 143 CH-53Es are being modified to the news standard by 2020.

Despite these extensive efforts the USMC struggles with maintaining an already middle aged aircraft fleet. Lack of spares and deep maintenance reduces the availability of aircraft dramatically.

The MV-22 Osprey fleet is going to achieve Full Operational Capability (FOC) sometime in 2020 despite having seen extensive service since 2007. Upgrades to the platform are being focused on improving communications, range, survivability and weapons. The communications issue is being addressed by the planned insertion of the Software Reprogrammable Payload (SRP) which will enhance digital connectivity across USMC assets in theatre. Further enhancements will see the Osprey receive Tactical Targeting Network Technology Link 16 and Common Data Link waveforms. 291 aircraft will also get Iridium SATCOM systems. Special attention has been made to aerial refuelling of the Ospreys from USAF's fleet of KC-10 and KC-46 tankers as well as USMC assets.

By 2019 a fully capable V-22 Aerial Refuelling system (VARS) will be available. This means that every Osprey could become an aerial tanker capable of delivering 4540 lbs of fuel to other aircraft. 345 Ospreys will receive this modification. 175 are to get Traffic Collision Avoidance Systems in a program that began in 2017. The readiness of the Osprey fleet has been a cause of concern to USMC planners for a number of years. To address this the Common Configuration Reliability and Modernisation (CCRAM) plan was put in place with the objective of improving availability by the order of 82 percent. This was harder to achieve than expected with 75 subtle variants of the basic V-22 design within the USMC's fleet of 360 aircraft.

The USMC's attack helicopters fleet comprises of Bell AH-1W Super Cobra and the AH-1Z Viper and the utility variant the venerable UH-1Y and AH-1Z is 85 percent of major components which has seen an improvement in stores holdings of spare parts for the machines. The older UH-1N Twin Huey has now been replaced in the USMC's inventory but the elderly Super Cobra still has 60 percent of the fleet but is steadily being replaced by the later Viper variant. Super Cobras removed from service are being offered up to foreign buyers.

USMC plans to acquire a total of 189 AH-1Zs and 160 UH-1Ys which will be spread between seven active squadrons. Each squadron will have 15 Vipers and 12 Y models. A second 'minus' reserve squadron with 12 and 9 aircraft respectively will also be supplied by a fleet replacement squadron with 30 Super Cobras.

In autumn 2018 the forward deployed 31st Marine Expeditionary Unit completed their transition to the Viper. Self defence for helicopters has been a focus of attention in recent years with the Viper having been armed for the first time with the new Joint Air to Ground missile in December 2017 as well as for the AIM-9X Sidewinder air-to-air missile.

Beyond 2030 the USMC plans to replace its fleet of H1s with a new aircraft developed by the Joint Vertical Lift Program. The new aircraft's primary role being to escort the MV-22 into what has been called 'destructed expeditionary operations from the sea'.

The USMC's vast array of aircraft is both its strength and its weakness. Too many elderly airframes means increased non-availability and heavy maintenance. Newer aircraft like the CH-53K King Stallion are making the availability better but it is an extremely tall order for the USMC to achieve the planned transformation of its entire rotary wing aviation fleet.

AIRCRAFT OF THE UNITED STATES NAVY
Squadron Numbers

Squadron Nickname	Squadron Nickname
FA-18 Super Hornet	**FA-18C Hornet**
VFA-2 BOUNTY HUNTERS	VFA-204 RIVER RATTLERS
VFA-11 RED RIPPERS	
VFA-14 TOPHATTERS	**F-35C Lightning**
VFA-22 FIGHTING REDCOCKS	
VFA-25 FIST OF THE FLEET	VFA-101 GRIM REAPERS
VFA-27 ROYAL MACES	VFA-125 ROUGH RIDERS
VFA-31 TOMCATTERS	VFA-147 ARGONAUTS
VFA-32 SWORDSMEN	
VFA-34 BLUE BLASTERS	**EA-18G Growler**
VFA-37 RAGIN BULLS	
VFA-41 BLACK ACES	VAQ-129 VIKINGS
VFA-83 RAMPAGERS	VAQ-130 ZAPPERS
VFA-81 SUNLINERS	VAQ-131 LANCERS
VFA-86 SIDEWINDERS	VAQ-132 SCORPIONS
VFA-87 GOLDEN WARRIORS	VAQ-133 WIZARDS
VFA-94 MIGHTY SHRIKES	VAQ-134 GARUDAS
VFA-97 WARHAWKS	VAQ-135 BLACK RAVENS
VFA-102 DIAMONDBACKS	VAQ-136 GAUNTLETS
VFA-103 JOLLY ROGERS	VAQ-137 ROOKS
VFA-105 GUNSLINGERS	VAQ-138 YELLOW JACKETS
VFA-106 GLADIATORS	VAQ-139 COUGARS
VFA-113 STINGERS	VAQ-140 PATRIOTS
VFA-115 EAGLES	VAQ-141 SHADOWHAWKS
VFA-122 FLYING EAGLES	VAQ-142 GRAY WOLVES
VFA-136 KNIGHT HAWKS	VAQ-209 STAR WARRIORS
VFA-137 KESTRELS	
VFA-143 PUKIN' DOGS	**E-2C/D Hawkeye**
VFA-146 BLUE DIAMONDS	
VFA-147 ARGONAUTS	VAW-113 BLACK EAGLES
VFA-151 FIGHTING VIGILANTES	VAW-115 LIBERTY BELLS
VFA-154 BLACK KNIGHTS	VAW-116 SUN KINGS
VFA-195 DAMBUSTERS	VAW-117 WALLBANGERS
VFA-211 FLYING CHECKMATES	VAW-120 RAY HAWKS
VFA-213 BLACK LIONS	VAW-121 BLUE TAILS
VFC-12 FLYING OMARS	VAW-123 SCREWTOPS
	VAW-125 BEAR ACES
	VAW-126 SEAHAWKS

Squadron	Nickname	Squadron	Nickname
C-2A Greyhound		**C-130 Hercules**	
VRC-30	PROVIDERS	VR-53	CAPITAL EXPRESS
VRC-30	(Det 1) HUSTLERS	VR-54	REVELLERS
VRC-30	(Det 2) ROUGHNECKS	VR-55	MINUTEMEN
VRC-30	(Det 3) CRUSADERS	VR-62	NOMADS
VRC-30	(Det 4) PURE HORSEPOWER	VR-64	CONDORS
VRC-30	(Det 5) PROVIDERS	**C-40A Clipper**	
E-6B Mercury		VR-56	GLOBEMASTERS
		VR-57	CONQUISTADORS
VQ-3	IRONMEN	VR-58	SUNSEEKERS
VQ-4	SHADOWS	VR-59	LONE STAR EXPRESS
VQ-7	ROUGHNECKERS	VR-61	ISLANDERS
P-8A Poseidon		**C-20A/D/G and C-37 Gulfstream**	
VP-1	SCREAMING EAGLES		
VP-4	SKINNY DRAGONS	VR-1	STAR LIFTERS
VP-5	MAD FOXES	VR-51	WINDJAMMERS
VP-8	TIGERS		
VP-9	GOLDEN EAGLES	**MV-22B Osprey**	
VP-10	RED LANCERS		
VP-16	WAR EAGLES	VRM-30	TITANS
VP-26	TRIDENTS	VRM-40	Unnamed as of 2018
VP-30	PRO'S NEST	VRM-50	Unnamed as of 2018
VP-45	PELICANS		
		SH-60F/HH-60H/SH-60B/ MH-60R/MH-60S Seahawk	
P-3/EP-3 Orion			
		HSC-2	FLEET ANGELS
VP-40	FIGHTING MARLINS	HSC-3	MERLINS
VP-46	GREY KNIGHTS	HSC-4	BLACK KNIGHTS
VP-62	BROADARROWS	HSC-5	NIGHT DIPPERS
VP-69	TOTEMS	HSC-6	INDIANS
VPU-2	WIZARDS	HSC-7	DUSTY DOGS
		HSC-8	EIGHT-BALLERS
MQ-4C Triton		HSC-9	TRIDENTS
		HSC-11	DRAGON SLAYERS
VUP-11	Unnamed as of 2018	HSC-12	GOLDEN FALCONS
VUP-19	BIG RED	HSC-14	CHARGERS

Squadron	Nickname		Squadron	Nickname
HSC-15	RED LIONS		**T-45 Goshawk**	
HSC-21	BLACKJACKS			
HSC-22	SEA KNIGHTS		VT-7	EAGLES
HSC-23	WILDCARDS		VT-9	TIGERS
HSC-25	ISLAND KNIGHTS		VT-21	FIGHTING REDHAWKS
HSC-26	CHARGERS		VT-22	GOLDEN EAGLES
HSC-28	DRAGON WHALES		VT-31	WISE OWLS
HSM-35	MAGICIANS		VT-35	STINGRAYS
HSM-37	EASYRIDERS		VT-86	SABREHAWKS
HSM-40	AIRWOLVES			
HSM-41	SEAHAWKS		**T-6A/B Texan II**	
HSM-46	GRANDMASTERS			
HSL-48	VIPERS		VT-2	DOER BIRDS
HSL-49	SCORPIONS		VT-3	RED KNIGHTS
HSM-51	WARLORDS		VT-6	SHOOTERS
HSM-60	JAGUARS		VT-10	WILDCATS
HSM-70	SPARTANS		VT-27	BOOMERS
HSM-71	RAPTORS		VT-28	RANGERS
HSM-72	PROUD WARRIORS			
HSM-73	INDIANS		**TH-57 Sea Ranger**	
HSM-74	SWAMP FOX			
HSM-75	WOLFPACK		HT-8	EIGHT BALLERS
HSM-77	SABERHAWKS		HT-18	VIGILANT EAGLES
HSM-78	BLUEHAWKS		HT-28	HELIONS
HSM-79	GRIFFINS			
HSC-84	RED WOLVES		**Operational Test & Evaluation**	
HSC-85	FIRE HAWKS			
			HX-21	BLACKJACK
MH-53D/E Sea Dragon			VX-1	PIONEERS
			VX-9	VAMPIRES
HM-12	SEA DRAGONS		VX-20	FORCE
HM-14	VANGUARD		VX-23	SALTY DOGS
HM-15	BLACKHAWKS		VX-30	BLOODHOUNDS
			VX-31	DUST DEVILS
MQ-8B/C Fire Scout			VXS-1	WARLOCKS
HSM-35	MAGICIANS			

Squadron Nickname	Squadron Nickname
F-5F/N Aggressors	
VFC-13 SAINTS	VFC-111 SUNDOWNERS

AIRCRAFT OF THE US MARINE CORPS
Squadron Numbers

The Marine Corps aviation is organised differently from the US Navy. There are four Marine Air Wings (MAW) and within each MAW there are three to four Marine Air Groups (MAG). Each MAG can be assigned any number of squadrons, each with differing roles and aircraft. In some cases aircraft can be drawn from individual squadrons and assigned to a composite squadron – so for example it is not unusual to see fixed wing Harrier aircraft assigned to a Heavy Lift Helicopter squadron. To make this second easier to read, where more than one type of aircraft is commonly assigned to a squadron, we have listed those squadrons by role, rather than aircraft type.

Squadron	Nickname	Squadron	Nickname
F-35B Lightning		VMFA(AW)-533	NIGHTHAWKS
		VMFAT-101	SHARPSHOOTERS
VMFA-121	GREEN KNIGHTS		
VMFA-122	FLYING LEATHERJACKETS	**AV-8 Harrier**	
VMFA-211	WAKE ISLAND AVENGERS	VMA-214	BLACK SHEEP
		VMA-223	BULLDOGS
VMFA-501	WARLORDS	VMA-231	ACE OF SPADES
		VMA-311	TOMCATS
FA-18 Hornet		VMA-542	TIGERS
		VMAT-203	HAWKS
VMFA-232	RED DEVILS		
VMFA-251	THUNDERBOLTS	**MV-22 Osprey**	
VMFA-312	CHECKERBOARDS		
VMFA-323	DEATH RATTLERS	VMM-161	GRAYHAWKS
VMFA(AW)-224	BENGALS	VMM-162	GOLDEN EAGLES
VMFA(AW)-225	VIKINGS	VMM-163	RIDGE RUNNERS
VMFA(AW)-242	BATS	VMM-164	KNIGHTRIDERS
		VMM-165	WHITE KNIGHTS

Squadron	Nickname	Squadron	Nickname
VMM-166	SEA ELK	**Unmanned Aerial Vehicles**	
VMM-261	RAGING BULLS		
VMM-262	FLYING TIGERS	VMU-1	WATCHDOGS
VMM-263	THUNDER EAGLES	VMU-2	NIGHT OWLS
VMM-264	BLACK KNIGHTS	VMU-3	PHANTOMS
VMM-265	DRAGONS	VMU-4	EVIL EYES
VMM-266	FIGHTING GRIFFINS	**Tanker and Transport**	
VMM-268	RED DRAGONS		
VMM-362	UGLY ANGELS	VMGR-152	SUMOS
VMM-363	RED LIONS	VMGR-234	RANGERS
VMM-364	PURPLE FOXES	VMGR-252	OTIS
VMM-365	BLUE KNIGHTS	VMGR-352	RAIDERS
VMM-764	MOONLIGHT	VMGR-452	YANKEES
VMM-774	WILD GOOSE		
VMM-204	RAPTORS	**Dissimilar Air Combat**	

Heavy Helicopter

VMFT-401   SNIPERS

HMH-361	FLYING TIGERS	**VIP Transport/Operational Test**	
HMH-366	HAMMERHEADS		
HMH-461	IRON HORSES	HMX-1	KNIGHTHAWKS
HMH-462	HEAVY HAULERS	VMR-1	ROADRUNNERS
HMH-463	PEGASUS	VMX-22	ARGONAUTS
HMH-464	CONDORS		
HMH-465	WAR HORSE		
HMH-466	WOLFPACK		
HMHT-302	PHOENIX		

Light/Attack Helicopter

HMLA-167	WARRIORS
HMLA-169	VIPERS
HMLA-267	STINGERS
HMLA-269	GUN RUNNERS
HMLA-367	SCARFACE
HMLA-369	GUNFIGHTERS
HMLA-469	VENGEANCE
HMLA-773	RED DOGS
HMLA-775	COYOTES
HMLAT-303	ATLAS

Lockheed F-35 LIGHTNING II

Variants: F-35B; F-35C
Role: Multi-role attack and fighter aircraft
Engines: Single Pratt & Whitney F-135 turbofan engine. 43,000 pounds max (in addition a Rolls-Royce/Allison shaft-driven lift-fan in F-35B)
Length: 15.4 metres (F-35B); 15.5 metres (F-35C) **Height:** 4.6 metres (F-35B); 4.7 metres (F-35C) **Wingspan:** 10.7 metres (F-35B); 13.1 metres (F-35C)
Weight: Maximum Take-off Gross Weight 22,680 kg
Airspeed: Mach 1.6 **Ceiling:** 50,000+ feet
Range: 450-600 nautical miles **Crew:** One
Armament: One external 25-mm GAU-12 gun pod; Four hardpoints in two internal weapon bays plus six external hardpoints for a mix of missiles and precision guided bombs.

Notes: The F-35 is the future of the USN/USMC fast jet fighter force and is the world's most expensive combat aircraft. A true fifth generation, single seat stealth multi-role aircraft the F-35 has been designed to conduct close air support, tactical bombing and air defence missions. The F-35 has three distinct variants with the USN/USMC operating two of them, the A variant is only operated by the US Air Force. The B variant, a Vertical Take Off and Landing variant, is being acquired for the US Marines for operation from Wasp and America class ships, whilst the F-35C is a carrier based variant and is fitted for operations with catapults and arrestor gear found on aircraft carriers. The US Marines first took possession of their first F-35Bs in April 2010, whilst the first F-35C was stood up in May 2012.

Boeing F/A-18 SUPER HORNET

Variants: F/A-18E; F/A-18F
Role: Multi-role attack and fighter aircraft
Engines: Two F414-GE-400 turbofan engines. 22,000 pounds (9,977 kg) static thrust per engine.
Length: 18.5 metres **Height:** 4.87 metres **Wingspan:** 13.68 metres
Weight: Maximum Take-off Gross Weight 29,932 kg
Airspeed: Mach 1.8+ **Ceiling:** 50,000+ feet
Range: Combat - 1,275 nautical miles, clean plus two AIM-9s; Ferry - 1,660 nautical miles, two AIM-9s, three 480 gallon tanks retained.
Crew: E model: one; F model: two.
Armament: One M61A1/A2 Vulcan 20mm cannon; AIM 9 Sidewinder, AIM-9X (projected), AIM 7 Sparrow, AIM-120 AMRAAM, Harpoon, Harm, SLAM, SLAM-ER (projected), Maverick missiles; Joint Stand-Off Weapon (JSOW); Joint Direct Attack Munition (JDAM); Data Link Pod; Paveway Laser Guided Bomb; Various general purpose bombs, mines and rockets

Notes: The F/A-18E/F provides the carrier strike group with a significantly powerful asset with a substantial amount of growth potential as well as enhanced range, endurance and ordnance carrying capability. The Super Hornet has now completely replaced the earliest A and B variants of the Hornet in service.

Boeing F/A-18 HORNET

Variants: F/A-18D
Role: All-weather attack and fighter aircraft
Engines: Two F404-GE-400 turbofan engines. 16,000 pounds static thrust each.
Length: 17.06 metres **Height:** 4.87 metres **Wingspan:** 11.43 metres
Airspeed: Mach 1.8+. **Ceiling:** 50,000+ feet
Range: Fighter mission - 400 nautical miles; Attack mission - 575 nautical miles;
Ferry - 2,000 nautical miles.
Crew: Two.
Armament: One M61A1/A2 Vulcan 20mm cannon; AIM 9 Sidewinder, AIM-9X, Maverick missiles, AIM-120 AMRAAM, Harpoon, Harm, SLAM, SLAM-ER, Joint Stand Off Weapon (JSOW), Joint Direct Attack Munition (JDAM), Data Link Pod, Paveway Laser Guided Bomb; Various general-purpose bombs, mines and rockets.

Notes: The A, B and C variants of the Hornet have been decommissioned from service and the D is gradually being replaced in service by the Super Hornet E/F variants or the F-35 Lightning II in service. The D variants are expected to remain in service with USN and USMC squadrons until 2023.

Grumman E-2 HAWKEYE

Variants: E-2C, E-2D
Role: Airborne Command & Control, Battle Space Management
Engines: Two Allison T-56-A427 turboprop engines; (5,100 shaft horsepower each)
Length: 17.5 metres **Height:** 5.6 metres **Wingspan:** 28 metres
Weight: Max. gross take-off: 53,000 lbs (23,850 kg) 40,200 lbs basic (18,090 kg)
Airspeed: 300+ knots **Ceiling:** 30,000 feet
Crew: Five (two pilots, three mission systems operators)

Notes: The Hawkeye is one of the first aircraft to launch from the flight deck of aircraft carriers at the start of any mission to allow them to get into position high above the battlespace in order to provide airborne early warning and command and control functions. The aircraft is one of the most distinctive aboard a carrier with its huge radome on the back of the fuselage. Ten fleet squadrons fly the Hawkeye. The E-2D variant is the latest in a long line of variants of the Hawkeye which can trace its lineage back to the late 1960s and first entered service with VAW-125 in March 2014. The E-2D Advanced Hawkeye benefits from having the non-rotating ALD-18 active electronically scanned (AESA) radar. In December 2016, an E-2D flew for the first time fitted with an aerial refuelling capability. This feature will allow the aircraft to double its time on station to five hours and increase total mission time from four to seven hours. The refuelling modification will start being built into the 46th plane (out of 75 planned) for delivery in late 2020 costing an additional US$2 million per aircraft, and the Navy plans to retrofit the feature on all previous Hawkeyes for US$6 million per plane.

Boeing EA-18G GROWLER

Variants: EA-18G
Role: Airborne Electronic Attack
Propulsion: Two General Electric F414-GE-400 engines (44,000 pounds thrust).
Length: 18.3 metres **Height:** 4.9 metres **Wingspan:** 13.7 metres
Weight: Empty Weight 33,094 pounds (15,011 kg); Max. Take-off Weight 66,000 lbs (29,964 kg); Recovery Weight 48,000 lbs (21,772 kg)
Airspeed: Mach 1.8 **Ceiling:** 50,000 feet
Range: 1,275+ nautical miles
Crew: 2 - Pilot and Weapon Systems Officer
Armament: ALQ-218 Tactical Receiver System; ALQ-99 Tactical Jamming System; AGM-88 HARM missiles; AIM-120 AMRAAM missile.

Notes: The EA-18G Growler is based on the battle proven F/A-18E/F Super Hornet Block II and conducts the airborne electronic attack mission. In this role the aircraft uses the proven capabilities of the latest AEA avionics suite evolved from the Improved Capability III (ICAP III) system. The majority of the sensors for this system are to be found on a pallet in the gun bay and in two wingtip pods. Each Growler has nine hardpoints for weapons, jamming pods and other stores such as communications countermeasures. The first flight of an EA-18G Growler took place on 10 September 2007. The Growler is being procured with a projected total force strength of 135 aircraft spread across 16 squadrons, with each squadron fielding eight aircraft.

Boeing AV-8B HARRIER

Variants: AV-8B; AV-8B II+; TAV-8B
Role: Day/Night ground attack
Engine: One Rolls Royce F402-RR-408 turbofan engine
Thrust: 23,400 pounds
Length: 14.11 metres **Wing span:** 9.24 metres
Airspeed: 650 knots (max) **Ceiling:** 50,000ft
Range: 1,200 nautical miles
Crew: 1
Armament: Mk-82 series 500lbs bombs, Mk-83 series 1000lbs bombs, GBU-12 500lbs laser guided bombs, GBU-16 1000lbs laser guided bombs, AGM-65F IR Maverick missiles, AGM-65E Laser Maverick missiles, CBU-99 cluster munitions, AIM-9M sidewinders, Litening II targeting POD to deliver GBU-12 and GBU-16 bombs with pinpoint accuracy.

Notes: AV-8B Harriers are operated from the large amphibious flat tops of the Wasp and America-class. The aircraft is based on the one designed by the British in the 1960s but contains significant differences from their Anglo counterparts. The prime mission of the AV-8B is to deliver knock out ground attacks in support of US Marine Corps operations. The two seat TAV-8B trainers underwent an upgrade that has equipped them with enhanced night vision goggle compatible lighting, new colour displays and a more powerful and reliable Rolls Royce Pegasus (408) engine. The AV-8B will progressively be replaced in service by Vertical Take Off and Landing F-35B Lightning although Harrier operations are expected to continue until at least 2025.

Sikorsky SH-60/MH-60 SEAHAWK

Variants: SH-60B; SH-60F; MH-60S; MH-60R; VH-60N
Role: ASW; Anti-shipping strike; SAR; Cargo Lift
Engines: Two General Electric T700-GE-700 or T700-GE-701C engines
Length: 19.6 metres **Height:** 3.9 to 5.1 metres **Rotor Diameter:** 16.4 metres
Weight: 21,000 to 23,000 pounds (9,450 to 10,350 kg)
Airspeed: 180 knots maximum
Range: Approx 380 nautical miles **Crew:** 3 - 4
Armament: Depending on a/c variant a combination of: 4-8 AGM-114 Hellfire missiles; M60 or M240 MG; GAU-17A Minigun; Up to three torpedoes; Airborne Mine Clearance System

Notes: The Sikorsky SH-60 Seahawk first entered US Navy service in 1979 and after forty years the type continues to be the mainstay of the American fleet. Through successive upgrades and redesigns the Seahawk remains current and hugely effective in all its various roles across the fleet. The MH-60R and MH-60S are multi-mission combat helicopters, deploy as companion squadrons embarked in aircraft carriers, surface warships and logistic ships. The R variant is equipped to provide surface and subsurface warfare support and is fitted with powerful low frequency dipping sonar to detect submerged submarines a well as electronic support measures, forward looking infrared (FLIR) and is armed with air-to-surface missiles. The S variant is a mine warfare support aircraft but can be configured to provide Combat Search and Rescue and Naval Special Warfare support. The R and S types will eventually replace the now somewhat elderly SH-60Bs and SH-60F helicopters in due course.

Sikorsky VH-60N WHITE HAWK

Variants: VH-60N
Role: Presidential and VIP Support
Engines: Two General Electric T-700-GE-401 turboshafts
Max. take-off weight: 23,501 lbs (10,660 kg)
Length: 19.76 metres **Height:** 5.13 metres
Airspeed: 159 knots **Ceiling:** 18,996 feet
Range: 1,379 nautical miles

Notes: 9 VH-60N White Hawk aircraft were produced in 1988 of which eight are still operational. Based on the basic UH-60 Black Hawk helicopter the VH-60N, these aircraft are likely to be replaced by new build Sikorsky VH-92A aircraft. In service, the President's helicopter is typically flanked by other VH-60Ns to disguise the actual helicopter carrying the American Commander-in-Chief. Pilots of VH-60N are dressed in their Blue Dress uniforms (as opposed to flight suits).

Sikorsky VH-92A KNIGHTHAWK

Variants: VH-92A
Role: Presidential and VIP Support
Engines: Two General Electric CT7-8A turboshaft engines, 2,520 shp each
Rotor diameter: 17.17 metres
Max. take-off weight: 27,700 lbs (12,568 kg)
Airspeed: 151 knots **Ceiling:** 14,000 feet
Range: 539 nautical miles
Crew: 2 **Capacity:** 19 passengers

Notes: These new aircraft will, from 2020, replace the 40-plus year old VH-3D Sea Kings operating as Presidential and VIP transports by the US Marine Corps. The VH-92A is based on the commercial S-92 helicopter but will only bear an external resemblance to their civilian cousins. Inside, the aircraft will be fitted to the specific requirements of Marine Corps Squadron HMX-1 and the US Secret Service including the fitting of armour plating and self-protection against surface-to-air missiles and heavy calibre machine gun ammunition. The VH-92A made its maiden flight at Sikorsky's plant at Stratford in Connecticut on 28 July 2017 and on 22 September 2018 made its first landing in the grounds of the White House during a test flight. Each of the projected 21 VH-92As to be procured will be able to be folded up and stowed inside a US Air Force C-5M Super Galaxy or C-17 Globemaster transport aircraft when the US President makes foreign visits. In addition to replacing the venerable Sea Kings the new VH-92As will also replace, in whole or in part, the fleet of VH-60N White Hawks operated by the USMC in the Presidential Support role.

Sikorsky CH-53 SEA STALLION

Variants: RH-53D; CH-53E
Role: Air Assault; Heavy transport
Engines: Three GE T64-GE-416 turboshaft engines producing 4,380 shp each:
Length 30.3 metres **Height:** 8.64 metres **Rotor diameter:** 24.07 metres
Airspeed: 150 knots
Maximum take-off weight: Internal load: 69,750 pounds (31,666 kg) External load: 73,500 pounds (33,369 kg)
Range: without refueling: 540 nautical miles; with aerial refueling: indefinite
Crew: 3
Armament: Two XM-218 .50 calibre machine guns

Notes: This heavy lift helicopter has been the mainstay of the USMC since the 1960s with the CH-53E being the latest and most powerful example of the type. The E variant is to be found operating from most amphibious ships and capable of lifting 16 tons of cargo or personnel over 50 nautical miles and returning. These aircraft are often seen lifting M198 howitzers or 26,000lb Light Armoured Vehicles. Such is the capability of the Sea Stallion that it is possible for one aircraft to retrieve another downed one.

Sikorsky CH-53K KING STALLION

Role: Air Assault; Heavy Transport
Engines: 3 x General Electric T408-GE-38-1B engines producing 7,500 shp each
Length: 30.2 metres **Height:** 8.46 metres **Rotor Diameter:** 24 metres
Max. take-off weight: 88,000 lbs
Airspeed: 170 knots
Range: 460 nautical miles
Armament: 2 window mounted .50 M3M/GAU-21 MG and a third MG mounted on the stern ramp
Crew: 5 - 2 pilots, 1 crew chief and 2 gunners

Notes: The Sikorsky CH-53K King Stallion is almost a brand-new aircraft type being introduced into the US Marine Corps to replace its legacy fleet of Sea Stallions. In April 2006 the USMC contracted for 156 of the new type, later increased to 227 which sees improvements over earlier models especially with new engines and cockpit layout. The K variant has nearly twice the lift capacity of the D and E Sea Stallion and twice the radius of action. Other enhancements have seen the widening of the cargo hold to allow the transportation of a Humvee vehicle inside. Despite this the helicopter will have a narrower footprint due to redesigned slimline composite sponsors. The helicopters will also have a new composite rotor blade system.The first flight of the CH-53K took place on 27 October 2015 with the first operational example of the type being delivered to the US Marine Corps on 16 May 2018. The second aircraft is scheduled for delivery in early 2019.

Sikorsky MH-53 SEA DRAGON

Variant: MH-53E
Role: Mine-countermeasures; Vertical Onboard Delivery
Engines: Three GE T64-GE-419 turboshaft engines producing 4,750 shp each
Length: Fuselage 22 metres; Overall 30.2 metres **Height:** 8.6 metres
Rotor Diameter: 24.1 metres
Weight: Max. Gross weight, w/external load: 69,750 lbs (31,693 kg); Empty weight 36,745 lb (16,667 kg)
Airspeed: 150 knots **Ceiling:** 10,000 feet.
Range: Max: 1,050 nautical miles.
Crew: Two pilots, one to six aircrewmen
Load: 55 troops or 32,000 pounds (14,512 kg) cargo

Notes: The Sea Dragon is heavier than the E variant of the Sea Stallion and has greater fuel reserves. These helicopters can transport up to 55 troops or a 16 tons payload over 50 miles. Some of the aircraft were fitted with extra armour and ramp mounted GAU-21 machine guns and night vision equipment. Currently the Sea Dragon is the main US Navy asset assigned to Airborne Mine Countermeasure (AMCM) for which the aircraft drag a heavy sled across a suspected minefield that is fitted with sensitive equipment designed to detect and neutralise any sea mines discovered. A secondary role for the Sea Dragon is that of Vertical Onboard Delivery (VOD) mission. The Sea Dragon will continue to perform the AMCM role until at least 2025.

Bell UH-1 IROQUOIS/VENOM

Variants: UH-1Y
Role: Assault; Medevac; Utility
Engines: Two General Electric T700-GE-401C turboshaft engines; 1,828 shp each
Length: 17.78 metres **Height:** 4.5 metres **Rotor Diameter:** 14.8 metres
Weight: Empty: 11,840 pounds (5,370 kg); Max. Take-off Weight: 18,500 pounds (8,390 kg).
Airspeed: 158 knots **Ceiling:** 20,000 feet **Range:** 129 miles with combat load
Sensor: Advanced Third Gen - FLIR Systems, Inc. BRITE Star Block II
Crew: Pilot, co-pilot, crew chief, gunner, plus 6 to 8 combat equipped troops
Armament: M-240 7.62mm MG or GAU-16 .50 calibre MG or the GAU-17 7.62mm automatic gun; 2 external stations for 70 mm Hydra 70 or APKWS II rockets.

Notes: The UH-1Y Venom is the latest in a long line of technology upgrades for the venerable helicopter that first saw service in the early 1950s. Key to the success of the Vemon is the new composite four bladed rotor system which is ballistically tolerant up to 23mm rounds. Upgrades were also made to the transmission, gears, engines and cockpit. The Vemon shares 85 percent commonality of parts with the AH-1Z Super Cobra. The upgrades have allowed the Venom to achieve greater logistic support, longer range and be more survivable in combat situation. Up to 160 new build aircraft are being delivered with the last expected to be accepted into service by 2021.

Bell AH-1 SUPER COBRA/VIPER

Variants: AH-1W; AH-1Z
Role: Attack helicopter
Engines: Two General Electric T700-GE-401 engines; 1,800 shp each
Length: 17.8 metres **Height:** 4.37 metres **Rotor Diameter:** 14.6 metres
Maximum take-off weight: 18,500 pounds (8,409 kg)
Airspeed: 160 knots
Range: 370 nautical miles **Ceiling:** 20,000 feet (6,000 metres)
Crew: 2
Sensor: Advanced Third Gen - FLIR Systems, Inc. BRITE Star Block II
Armament: One 20mm turreted cannon with 750 rounds; Six external wing stations that can fire 2.75-inch or 5-inch rockets and a wide variety of precision guided missiles, including Hellfire (point target/anti-armour) and Sidewinder air-to-air missiles.

Notes: The AH-1Z is the latest incarnation of the long-established Bell Viper attack helicopter which provides the USMC with close air support, anti-armour, armed escort, armed/visual reconnaissance and fire support missions. The four bladed rotor system is what differentiates the Z variant from previous versions of the Viper which is gradually replacing on front line duties. 189 aircraft are being acquired which will be a mix of new build machines and conversions of existing AH-1Ws.

Bell-Boeing MV-22 OSPREY

Variants: MV-22; MV-22B
Role: Assault transport for troops, equipment and supplies
Engines: Two pivoting Rolls-Royce/Allison AE1107C engines
Rotor Diameter: 11.58 metres **Blades per rotor:** Three
Weight: 60,500 lbs max
Airspeed: 272 knots **Ceiling:** 25,000 feet
Crew: 3 **Capacity:** 24 troops
Avionics: AAQ-16 FLIR; AAR-47 missile warning system; APR-39A(V)2 EW
Armament: One 7.62mm or one 12.7mm MG firing from the rear ramp

Notes: This unique type of aircraft was under development for many years and suffered several publicly damaging crashes during its early stages. The MV-22 can carry 24 fully equipped troops into action much quicker than a comparable helicopter or a 10,000 lbs external load. The aircraft has a range of 2,100 nautical miles with a single inflight refuelling. The Osprey has been gradually replacing the CH-53E Sea Stallion in service across the fleet and production is set at 24-48 aircraft annually.
Twelve 'Green Top' MV-22Bs are allocated to HMX-1 Squadron at Quantico, Virginia to provide Presidential and VIP transport and support. The first Osprey in this role was delivered in May 2013. They support White House travels by shuttling essential personnel and VIPs, although the aircraft are unlikely to transport the President but in December 2018 carried Melania Trump, the First Lady, on a visit to the aircraft carrier USS GEORGE H. W. BUSH.

Sikorsky VH-3D SEA KING

Variants: VH-3D
Role: Presidential and VIP Support
Engines: Two General Electric T58-GE-400B turboshaft engines
Weight: 21,500 lbs max
Airspeed: 140 knots
Crew: 2 pilots; 1 crew chief

Notes: These venerable aircraft are operated by HMX-1 from the US Marine Corps base at Quantico in Virginia. They are the last examples of the Sea King operating in the United States. They are capable of operations in all weather conditions and are equipped with a high level of redundant systems. When the American President is on board they are referred to as 'Marine One'. These aircraft will be replaced by the Sikorsky VH-92A from 2020.

Lockheed P-3 ORION

Variants: P-3C; EP-3E
Role: ASW; Maritime Patrol; Recce and Intelligence Collection
Engines: Four Allison T-56-A-14 turboprop engines (4,900 shp each)
Length: 35.57 metres **Height:** 10.27 metres **Wingspan:** 30.36 metres
Weight: Max. gross take-off: 139,760 pounds (63,394.1 kg)
Airspeed: Maximum - 411 knots; Cruise - 328 knots **Ceiling:** 28,300 feet
Range: Maximum mission range - 2,380 nautical miles; For three hours on station at 1,500 feet - 1,346 nautical miles
Crew: 11 (22 EP-3E)
Armament: 20,000 pounds (9 metric tons) of ordnance including: Harpoon (AGM-84D) cruise missiles, SLAM (AGM-84E) missiles, Maverick (AGM 65) air-to-ground missiles, MK-46/50 torpedoes, rockets, mines, depth bombs, and special weapons.

Notes: First flown in 1961 the P-3 Orion is gradually being phased out of service within the US Navy and replaced by the Boeing P-8 Poseidon. The P-3 Orions, however, still perform a valuable service conducting anti-submarine, reconnaissance and intelligence gathering missions. Their economic turboprop engines allow the aircraft to loiter over an area for an extended period. The 16-strong EP-3E fleet of intelligence gathering aircraft underwent an upgrade in the early 2010s that saw the installation of sensitive receivers and high gain dish antennas with which they are able to monitor a wide range of electronic emissions from deep within targeted territory.

Boeing P-8 POSEIDON

Variants: P-8A
Role: ASW and Anti-Surface Warfare
Engines: Two high-bypass turbofan engines (CFM-56)
Length: 39.47 metres **Height:** 12.83 metres **Wingspan:** 35.72 metres
Weight: Max. gross take-off: 184,200 pounds (83,553 kg)
Airspeed: 490 knots **Ceiling:** 41,000 feet
Range: Maximum mission range - 1,200 nautical miles; For four hours on station
Crew: 9
Armament: Five internal and six external hardpoints (four wing and two centreline mounted) all supported by digital stores management allowing for the carriage of missiles, torpedoes and mines. Sonobuoys are deployed via a rotary reloadable, pneumatically controlled launcher.

Notes: Designed to replace the elderly Lockheed P-3 Orion in service and based on the Boeing Next Generation 737-800 series aircraft. The US Navy plans to acquire 117 P-8A and is active in promoting the sale of this type to friendly foreign nations including New Zealand, Australia, India, the United Kingdom and Norway.

Boeing E-6 MERCURY

Variant: E-6B
Role: Communications Relay and Strategic Airborne Command Post
Engines: Four CFM-56-2A-2 high bypass turbofan engines
Length: 45.8 metres **Height:** 12.9 metres **Wingspan:** 45.2 metres
Weight: Max. Gross take-off: 341,000 lbs (153,900 kg)
Airspeed: Approximately 522 knots
Ceiling: 40,000+ feet **Range:** 6,600 nautical miles
Crew: 22

Notes: Originally designed to provide the TACAMO (Take Charge and Move Out) role, providing emergency command and control of fleet ballistic missile submarines. The new E-6E aircraft have now added to this role that of Airborne Command Post and becoming a dual role aircraft in the process. This aircraft allows the US Commander in Chief and his Defense Secretary to be in contact with submarines, bombers and missile silos.

Grumman C-2 GREYHOUND

Variant: C-2A
Role: Carrier On-board Delivery (COD) aircraft
Engines: Two Allison T56-A-425 turboprop engines; 4,600 shp each
Length: 17.3 metres   **Height:** 5.28 metres   **Wingspan:** 24.56 metres
Weight: Max. Gross take-off: 57,500 lbs (26,082 kg)
Airspeed: Cruise - approximately 260 knots; Max. - approximately 343 knots
Ceiling: 30,000 feet   **Range:** 1,300 nautical miles
Crew: 4

Notes: These aircraft were developed from the E-2 Hawkeye. Greyhounds provide aircraft carriers with the critical logistics support. The primary mission of the C-2A Greyhound is the transport of high priority cargo, mail and passengers to deployed aircraft carriers and shore bases. The aircraft can carry a maximum payload of 10,000 lbs and the cabin area can be quickly reconfigured to accommodate cargoes or passengers or stretcher medical cases. To keep the cargoes from moving whilst in flight the cabin is configured with a cargo cage system with strong restraints, which is particularly useful during landings or catapult launches. Each C-2A Greyhound has a large cargo ramp at the stern of the aircraft as well as a powered winch to pull large/heavy loads into the cabin. The C-2A fleet underwent a Service Life Extension (SLEP) that included structural enhancements, rewiring, improvements to the avionics and new propeller systems. In 2015 the US Navy selected the V-22 Osprey as the basis for the C-2A Greyhound's eventual replacement in the fleet. The US Navy has scheduled the ordering of four Ospreys each year from fiscal year 2018 to 2020. The USMC will be responsible for training the Navy pilots in the use of Ospreys in the future.

Northrop Grumman MQ-4C TRITON

Variant: MQ-4C
Role: Persistent Maritime Intelligence, Surveillance & Reconnaissance (ISR)
Engines: Rolls-Royce AE3007H
Length: 14.5 metres **Height:** 4.7 metres **Wingspan:** 39.9 metres
Weight: Max. Gross take-off: 32,250 lbs (14,628 kg)
Airspeed: 310 knots **Endurance:** 30 hours
Ceiling: 60,000 feet **Range:** 9,950 nautical miles
Crew: Four per ground station

Notes: Developed under the Broad Area Maritime Surveillance (BAMS) program this aircraft provides combat information to operational and tactical users such as Expeditionary Strike Group (ESG), Carrier Strike Group (CSG) and the Joint Forces Maritime Component Commander (JFMCC). The MQ-4C Triton is an unmanned aerial vehicle that is controlled by a data link back to ground stations that control and monitor its mission. The aircraft are forward deployed, land based and autonomous making it ideal for the role of persistent maritime ISR. Each aerial vehicle is equipped with a wealth of highly sensitive equipment. Operational capability commenced in 2017 and the US Navy eventually intends to purchase a total of up to 68 MQ-4C Tritons.

BOEING MQ-25 STINGRAY

Variants: MQ-25
Role: Unmanned Combat Air System
Engines: one Rolls Royce AE-3007N turbofan engine delivering 10,000 lb (4,500 kg)
Weight: Max. Gross take off; 44,533 lbs (20,200 kg)
Length: 19 metres **Height:** 3.5 metres
Airspeed: 335 knots **Ceiling:** 39,370 feet (12,000 metres)
Range: 2,485 miles

Notes: The US Navy's X-47B Unmanned Combat Air System (UCAS) program set out the somewhat daunting challenge of designing, developing and fielding a tailless, fighter sized unmanned aircraft which can be operated from the deck of aircraft carriers whilst underway at sea. The first aircraft to be trialled was the Northrop Grumman X-47B UCAS, but after a promising start Northrop Grumman withdrew its interest in developing the concept further in 2017.

The US Navy instead has devoted its attention on the MQ-25 Stingray in the role of aerial refuelling drone under the Carrier Based Aerial Refuelling System (CBARS) program, which had previously been known as the Unmanned Carrier Launched Airborne Surveillance and Strike (UCLASS) program. In July 2016 the aircraft was named MQ-25A Stingray. Under the auspices of the program the US Navy will develop the drone into an aerial refuelling aircraft that is expected to be a more capable and cost-effective solution than modifying F-35, V-22 Osprey or E-2D into the role. Despite this focus the Stingray will also be able to fire missiles or drop bombs from drop tank pylons, but this will be a definite secondary capability. The prototype was unveiled on

19 December 2017. On 30 August 2018, Boeing was awarded a US$805 million development contract for the construction and delivery of four MQ-25A aircraft to be completed by August 2024. The fleet is expected to eventually total 72 aircraft at a cost of US$13 billion.

The US Navy and US Marine Corps also operate a variety of smaller drones. 178 AeroVironment RQ-11B Ravens, otherwise known as Shadow 200 are small Remote Scouting Systems (SURSS) mid-range UAS (Unmanned Aerial Systems). 143 AeroVironment RQ-12A Wasp IV is another SURSS hand launched UAS weighing less than 3lbs in weight.

There are also 7 Insitu RQ-21A Blackjack UASs with a service ceiling of 20,000ft that provide commanders with day and night intelligence, surveillance and communication relay capabilities. Finally, there are 131 AeroVironment RQ-20B Pumas. These are the largest small SURSSs weighing 13.5lbs and with a range of 11 nautical miles and a service ceiling of 15,000ft.

Northrop Grumman MQ-8 FIRE SCOUT

Variants: MQ-8B; MQ-8C
Role: Unmanned Aerial Vehicle for Organic Surveillance
Engines: One Rolls-Royce 250C20W heavy fuel turboshaft engine
Length: 31.7 ft **Height:** 9.8 ft
Weight: 2,073 lbs (empty); 3,150 lbs max. take-off
Airspeed: 110 knots **Ceiling:** 20,000 feet
Load: 600 pounds, including electro-optical/infra-red sensor and laser

Notes: In November 2009 Northrop Grumman delivered the first three production models of this innovative aircraft design. Known as the Fire Scout Vertical Take-off and Landing Tactical Unmanned Air Vehicle (VTUAV) the vehicle is designed to be able to operate from any air capable warship. In October 2014 the MQ-8C, an upgraded version of the initial concept, based on the Bell 407 Jetranger airframe, made its first flight. The US Navy has a requirement for 30 of these surveillance aircraft. The US Navy and US Marine Corps operate a wide variety of fixed wing UAVs in a wide number of roles including, but not exclusive to, surveillance and strike roles. Aircraft in the inventory include the RQ-7B Raven, RQ-20A Puma and the RQ-21A Blackjack.

Boeing C-40 CLIPPER

Variants: C-40A
Role: Logistics Support
Engines: Two CFM56-7B SLST turbofans
Length: 33.63 metres **Height:** 12.55 metres **Wingspan:** 34.3 metres
Weight: Maximum take-off weight is 171,000 pounds
Airspeed: 585 - 615mph **Ceiling:** 41,000 feet
Range: 3,000+ nm with 121 passengers or 40,000 lbs of cargo
Crew: 4

Notes: These aircraft are based on the commercial Boeing 737 airliner design but modified for military use. They are operated by the USN Reserve and provide invaluable transportation support to the USN. The Clipper fleet was delivered from April 2001 and provides passenger and limited cargo transport around the world. The USN still has a small number of earlier types in its inventory including the C-12 Huron for short haul cargo transfer and VIP/Passenger transport operations. There are also a small number of C-20/C-37 Gulfstream aircraft which service in the executive transport role alongside a small number of UC-35 Cessna jets.

Lockheed C-130 HERCULES

Variants: C-130T; KC-130T; KC-130J
Role: Global airlift and inflight refuelling
Propulsion: Four Allison AE2100-D3 turboprops, each 4,591 shp *(details for KC-130J)*
Length: 29.79 metres **Height:** 11.81 metres **Wingspan:** 40.38 metres
Weight: Maximum take-off weight 164,000 pounds (74,389 kg)
Airspeed: 391 mph at 20,000 feet
Ceiling: 33,000 feet with 100,000 lbs (45,000 kg) payload
Range: 3,740 nautical miles with 20,000 lbs (9,072 kg) payload
Crew: Four: 2 Pilots, 2 Crewmen; up to 92 troops
Armament: Harvest Hawk - 1 x 30mm Bushmaster Cannon; 4 x Hellfire missiles; 10 x Griffin missiles

Notes: These venerable aircraft are used in a wide range of support roles across the USN and USMC spectrum including but not limited to transport and logistics support and launching aerial drones. The J variant is the latest example of the Hercules that has been in service in one form or another since the 1960s with the USN, USMC and US Air Force. The J offers increased capacity, longer range and enhanced avionics over its earlier examples. It can also be fitted exclusively for the air-to-air refuelling role. The USMC went further converting ten KC-130Js into a combination surveillance platform and gunships. The renamed KC-130J 'Harvest Hawk' retained the wing mounted refuelling pods and tanker mission but added a new targeting sensor and a 30mm Bushmaster cannon, which was mounted to fire sideways through the troop door. The final Harvest Hawk example was delivered in June 2014.

Boeing T-45C GOSHAWK

Variants: T-45C
Role: Training platform for Navy/Marine Corps pilots
Engine: Rolls Royce F405-RR-401 turbofan engine with 5,527 pounds thrust
Length: 11.98 metres   **Height:** 4.11 metres   **Wingspan:** 9.39 metres
Weight: Maximum Gross Take-off, 13,500 pounds (6,075 kg); empty 9,394 pounds (4,261 kg)
Airspeed: 645 mph   **Ceiling:** 42,500 feet
Range: 700 nautical miles (805 statute miles, 1,288 km)
Crew: Two (instructor and student pilot)
Armament: None

Notes: The T-45 Goshawk was developed from the successful British Hawk series of fast jet trainers that has become the standard advanced jet trainer within the US Navy and US Marine Corps. The first T-45 Goshawk became operational in 1991 and has been progressively upgraded from its original configuration which featured an analogue style cockpit and flight controls. Most of the aircraft have now been fitted with modern 'glass cockpit' design similar to those that equip front line Super Hornets and F-35 Lightning II aircraft.

Raytheon T-6 TEXAN II

Variants: T-6A; T-6B
Role: All-purpose turbo-prop trainer
Propulsion: One Pratt & Whitney Canada PT-6A-68 turboprop engine; 1,100 hp
Length: 10.12 metres **Height:** 3.29 metres **Wingspan:** 10.18 metres
Weight: Empty, 5,000 pounds (2,268 kg.); maximum take-off weight 6,500 pounds (2,948 kg)
Airspeed: 270 knots at 1,000 feet level flight **Ceiling:** 31,000 feet
Range: 900 nautical miles
Crew: Two (instructor and student pilot)

Notes: The Texan is a derivative of the Swiss Pilatus PC-9 but fitted with a Pratt and Whitney PT-6A-68 engine, revised cockpit layout and a Martin Baker ejection seat. The aircraft is laid out as a tandem seat trainer. The type was introduced into service in 2002 for student pilot training. In 2007 the B variant of the aircraft came off the production lines and featured a number of improvements over its earlier incarnation including a glass cockpit with three multi-function displays, a heads-up display and improved open architecture avionics which will allow future upgrades to be made with much greater ease. Delivery of the last of 252 T-6Bs was made in June 2016. The US Navy also operates a number of twin engine Raytheon T-44A/C Pegasus aircraft, which are operated by VT-31 Wise Owls at Naval Air Station Corpus Christi, Texas.

Bell H-57 SEA RANGER

Variants: TH-57B/C
Role: Flying training
Engine: One Allison 250-C20BJ turbofan engine
Length: Fuselage - 9.44 metres; Rotors turning - 11.9 metres
Height: 3.04 metres
Rotor Diameter: 10.78 metres
Weight: Empty 1595 pounds (725kg), maximum take-off 3200 pounds (1455 kg)
Airspeed: 138 mph; 117 mph cruising **Ceiling:** 18,900 feet
Range: 368 nautical miles
Crew: One pilot, four students

Notes: The TH-57 Sea Ranger is a militarised version of the commercial Bell Jet Ranger 206. The 45 B variant is used primarily for primary visual flight rules training whilst the 71 C examples are used for advanced instrument flight rules training. Both these types are operated by two training squadrons at NAS Whiting Field, Milton, Florida. A pair of these helicopters are operated at the Naval Air Warfare Center Aircraft Division at Patuxent River, Maryland conducting photo, chase and utility missions.

Eurocopter UH-72A LAKOTA

Variant: UH-72A
Role: Training Helicopter for US Naval Test Pilots School
Engine: 2 x Turbomeca Ariel 1E2 turboshafts
Length : 13.03 metres **Height:** 3.45 metres
Weight: Empty 3,950 lb; Maximum take-off weight 7,903 lb
Airspeed: Max. 145 Knots **Ceiling:** 18,000 feet **Range:** 370 nautical miles
Crew: Two (instructor and student pilot)

Notes: The US Navy version of this Eurocopter design is based on that owned and operated by the US Army. The first naval versions entered service in November 2009 and the last in January 2010. The aircraft are used by the US Navy Test Pilot School (USNTPS) for rotary wing curriculum activities.

Northrop Grumman F-5 TIGER

Variant: F-5N (single seat); F-5F (twin seat)
Role: Simulated Air-to-Air Combat Training
Engine: Two J85-GE-21C turbojet engines; 5,000 pounds (2,273 kg) of thrust each
Length: 14.4 metres **Height:** 4.1 metres **Wingspan:** 8.1 metres (figures for F-5N)
Weight: 24,722 lbs, empty; approx. 9,723 lb max.
Airspeed: Max: Mach 1.64 **Ceiling:** 50,000+ Feet
Range: Approximately 2,314 nautical miles
Crew: F-5N - One; F-5F - Two

Notes: The F-5N is a single seat, twin engine, tactical fighter or ground attack aircraft that provides simulated air-to-air combat for student and refreshing aerial combat training. The aircraft were manufactured by Northrop Grumman Corporation. The slightly larger F-5F is a twin seat version and serves in a similar role. The USN also has ownership of early generation F-16 Fighting Falcons that also serve in the Aggressor role that are primarily assigned to The Naval Strike and Air Warfare Center (Top Gun) located at NAS Fallon, Nevada, with detachments at Key West, Florida and MCAS Yuma, Arizona. In 2015 extra F-5N/F aircraft were acquired from the Swiss Air Force and these replaced aircraft with high flight hours.

UNITED STATES COAST GUARD

The role of the United States Coast Guard is a huge one; not only protecting the thousands of miles of coastline of the mainland United States but also Puerto Rico, Hawaii and Alaska. Furthermore following the terrorist attacks on 11 September 2001 the US Coast Guard has taken on a large portion of the responsibility for homeland security. The traditional roles of the service, namely, search and rescue, drug/illegal immigrant interdiction, reconnaissance and surveillance, environmental control, maintenance of river navigation aids and US law enforcement, remain.

To achieve this massive task the service employs 42,000 men and women of all ages and ranks taken from all walks of life. The US Coast Guard is unique in its structure as it is a military service and is an arm of the US Armed Forces. Established in 1915 the service has grown out of all proportions to its initial force structure and now extends its influence across the globe.

The US Coast Guard has in recent years seen the results of major investment in new vessels and equipment with the introduction into service of the new Bertholf-class, Sentinel and Famous-class cutters, but the service still has some extremely old vessels in its inventory, some of which date back as far as the Second World War. Another area of concern for the US Coast Guard is its continued operations in ice covered areas of the North around Alaska and in the Antarctic where in 2018 air operations, recommenced after a gap of many years. The elderly icebreakers that make up the fleet are old and worn out, and although President Trump has signalled his support for their replacement no new funds to build a new vessel of the type have, as yet been allocated.

US Coast Guard aviation is limited to helicopters and Hercules transport aircraft. The latter type caused concern for the leadership of the Coast Guard after a fatal crash left the fleet of C-130s grounded for a while.

In the coming years the US Coast Guard will see the withdrawal from service of the venerable 1960s built High Endurance Cutters and the 1970s Island Class replaced with newer, more economical and more sophisticated Large Security Cutters and the new Sentinel-class cutters.

SHIPS OF
THE UNITED STATES COAST GUARD

Ship	Hull Number	Ship	Hull Number
Medium Security Cutter		DECISIVE	WMEC 629
		ALERT	WMEC 630
BERTHOLF	WMSL 750	BEAR	WMEC 901
WAESCHE	WMSL 751	TAMPA	WMEC 902
STRATTON	WMSL 752	HARRIET LANE	WMEC 903
HAMILTON	WMSL 753	NORTHLAND	WMEC 904
JAMES	WMSL 754	SPENCER	WMEC 905
MUNRO	WMSL 755	SENECA	WMEC 906
KIMBALL	WMSL 756	ESCANABA	WMEC 907
MIDGETT	WMSL 757	TAHOMA	WMEC 908
STONE	WMSL 758	CAMPBELL	WMEC 909
Unnamed	WMSL 759	THETIS	WMEC 910
Unnamed	WMSL 760	FORWARD	WMEC 911
		LEGARE	WMEC 912
High Endurance Cutter		MOHAWK	WMEC 913
MELLON	WHEC 717	**Icebreakers**	
MUNRO	WHEC 724		
MIDGETT	WHEC 726	POLAR STAR	WAGB 10
		POLAR SEA	WAGB 11
Medium Endurance Cutter		HEALY	WAGB 20
		MACKINAW	WAGB 30
RELIANCE	WMEC 615	ALEX HALEY	WAGB 39
DILIGENCE	WMEC 616		
VIGILANT	WMEC 617	**Fast Response Cutter**	
ACTIVE	WMEC 618		
CONFIDENCE	WMEC 619	BERNARD C. WEBBER	WPC 1101
RESOLUTE	WMEC 620	RICHARD ETHERIDGE	WPC 1102
VALIANT	WMEC 621	WILLIAM FLORES	WPC 1103
STEADFAST	WMEC 623	ROBERT YERED	WPC 1104
DAUNTLESS	WMEC 624	MARGARET NORVELL	WPC 1105
VENTUROUS	WMEC 625	PAUL CLARK	WPC 1106
DEPENDABLE	WMEC 626	CHARLES DAVID	WPC 1107
VIGOROUS	WMEC 627	CHARLES SEXTON	WPC 1108

Ship	Hull Number	Ship	Hull Number
KATHLEEN MOORE	WPC 1109	CLARENCE SUTPHIN	WPC 1147
RAYMOND EVANS	WPC 1110	PABLO VALENT	WPC 1148
WILLIAM TRUMP	WPC 1111	DOUGLAS DENMAN	WPC 1149
ISAAC MAYO	WPC 1112	WILLIAM CHADWICK	WPC 1150
RICHARD DIXON	WPC 1113	WARREN DEYAMPERT	WPC 1151
HERIBERTO HERNANDEZ		MAURICE JESTER	WPC 1152
	WPC 1114	JOHN PATTERSON	WPC 1153
JOSEPH NAPIER	WPC 1115	WILLIAM SPARLING	WPC 1154
WILLIAM GRIESSER	WPC 1116	Unnamed	WPC 1155
RICHARD PATTERSON	WPC 1117	Unnamed	WPC 1156
JOSEPH TEZANOS	WPC 1118	Unnamed	WPC 1157
ROLLIN FRITCH	WPC 1119		
LAWRENCE LAWSON	WPC 1120	**Offshore Patrol Cutter**	
JOHN McCORMICK	WPC 1121		
BAILEY BARCO	WPC 1122	ARGUS	WMSM 915
BENJAMIN DAILEY	WPC 1123	CHASE	WMSM 916
DONALD HORSELEY	WPC 1124	INGHAM	WMSM 917
JACOB POROO	WPC 1125	RUSH	WMSM 918
JOSEPH GERCZAK	WPC 1126	PICKERIN	WMSM 919
RICHARD SNYDER	WPC 1127	ICARUS	WMSM 920
NATHAN BRUCKENTHAL	WPC 1128	ACTIVE	WMSM 921
FORREST O. REDNOUR	WPC 1129	DILIGENCE	WMSM 922
ROBERT G. WARD	WPC 1130	ALERT	WMSM 923
TERREL HORNE	WPC 1131	VIGILANT	WMSM 924
BENJAMIN A. BOTTOMS	WPC 1132	RELIANCE	WMSM 925
JOSEPH O. DOYLE	WPC 1133		
WILLIAM C. HART	WPC 1134	**Patrol Boats**	
ANGELA McSHAN	WPC 1135		
DANIEL TARR	WPC 1136	MAUI	WPB 1304
EDGAR CULBERTON	WPC 1137	OCRACOKE	WPB 1307
HAROLD MILLER	WPC 1138	AQUIDNECK	WPB 1309
MRYTLE HAZARD	WPC 1139	MUSTANG	WPB 1310
OLIVER HENRY	WPC 1140	NAUSHON	WPB 1311
CHARLES MOULTHROP	WPC 1141	SANIBEL	WPB 1312
ROBERTY GOLDMAN	WPC 1142	BARANOF	WPB 1318
FREDERICK HATCH	WPC 1143	CHANDELEUR	WPB 1319
GLENN HARRIS	WPC 1144	CUTTYHUNK	WPB 1322
EMLEN TUNNELL	WPC 1145	KEY LARGO	WPB 1324
JOHN SCHEUERMAN	WPC 1146	MONOMOY	WPB 1326
		SITKINAK	WPB 1329

Ship	Hull Number	Ship	Hull Number
TYBEE	WPB 1330	ADELIE	WPB 87333
WASHINGTON	WPB 1331	GANNET	WPB 87334
WRANGELL	WPB 1332	NARWHAL	WPB 87335
ADAK	WPB 1333	STURGEON	WPB 87336
LIBERTY	WPB 1334	SOCKEYE	WPB 87337
ANACAPA	WPB 1335	IBIS	WPB 87338
KISKA	WPB 1336	POMPANO	WPB 87339
BARRACUDA	WPB 87301	HALIBUT	WPB 87340
HAMMERHEAD	WPB 87302	BONITO	WPB 87341
MAKO	WPB 87303	SHRIKE	WPB 87342
MARLIN	WPB 87304	TERN	WPB 87343
STINGRAY	WPB 87305	HERON	WPB 87344
DORADO	WPB 87306	WAHOO	WPB 87345
OSPREY	WPB 87307	FLYING FISH	WPB 87346
CHINOOK	WPB 87308	HADDOCK	WPB 87347
ALBACORE	WPB 87309	BRANT	WPB 87348
TARPON	WPB 87310	SHEARWATER	WPB 87349
COBIA	WPB 87311	PETREL	WPB 87350
HAWKSBILL	WPB 87312	SEALION	WPB 87352
CORMORANT	WPB 87313	SKIPJACK	WPB 87353
FINBACK	WPB 87314	DOLPHIN	WPB 87354
AMBERJACK	WPB 87315	HAWK	WPB 87355
KITTIWAKE	WPB 87316	SAILFISH	WPB 87356
BLACKFIN	WPB 87317	SAWFISH	WPB 87357
BLUEFIN	WPB 87318	SWORDFISH	WPB 87358
YELLOWFIN	WPB 87319	TIGER SHARK	WPB 87359
MANTA	WPB 87320	BLUE SHARK	WPB 87360
COHO	WPB 87321	SEA HORSE	WPB 87361
KINGFISHER	WPB 87322	SEA OTTER	WPB 87362
SEAHAWK	WPB 87323	MANATEE	WPB 87363
STEELHEAD	WPB 87324	AHI	WPB 87364
BELUGA	WPB 87325	PIKE	WPB 87365
BLACKTIP	WPB 87326	TERRAPIN	WPB 87366
PELICAN	WPB 87327	SEA DRAGON	WPB 87367
RIDLEY	WPB 87328	SEA DEVIL	WPB 87368
COCHITO	WPB 87329	CROCODILE	WPB 87369
MANOWAR	WPB 87330	DIAMONDBACK	WPB 87370
MORAY	WPB 87331	REEF SHARK	WPB 87371
RAZORBILL	WPB 87332		

Ship	Hull Number	Ship	Hull Number
ALLIGATOR	WPB 87372	WILLIAM TATE	WLM 560
SEA DOG	WPB 87373	HARRY CLAIBORNE	WLM 561
SEA FOX	WPB 87374	MARIA BRAY	WLM 562
		HENRY BLAKE	WLM 563
Sail Training Ship		GEORGE COBB	WLM 564
EAGLE	WIX 327	**Inland Buoy Tenders**	
Seagoing Buoy Tenders		BLUEBELL	WLI 313
		BUCKTHORN	WLI 642
JUNIPER	WLB 201	BAYBERRY	WLI 65400
WILLOW	WLB 202	ELDERBERRY	WLI 65401
KUKUI	WLB 203		
ELM	WLB 204	**Construction Tenders Inland**	
WALNUT	WLB 205		
SPAR	WLB 206	SMILAX	WLIC 315
MAPLE	WLB 207	PAMLICO	WLIC 800
ASPEN	WLB 208	HUDSON	WLIC 801
SYCAMORE	WLB 209	KENNEBEC	WLIC 802
CYPRESS	WLB 210	SAGINAW	WLIC 803
OAK	WLB 211	ANVIL	WLIC 75301
HICKORY	WLB 212	HAMMER	WLIC 75302
FIR	WLB 213	SLEDGE	WLIC 75303
HOLLYHOCK	WLB 214	MALLET	WLIC 75304
SEQUOIA	WLB 215	VISE	WLIC 75305
ALDER	WLB 216	CLAMP	WLIC 75306
		HATCHET	WLIC 75309
Coastal Buoy Tenders		AXE	WLIC 75310
IDA LEWIS	WLM 551	**River Buoy Tenders**	
KATHERINE WALKER	WLM 552		
ABBIE BURGESS	WLM 553	OUACHITA	WLR 65501
MARCUS HANNA	WLM 554	CIMARRON	WLR 65502
JAMES RANKIN	WLM 555	OBION	WLR 65503
JOSHUA APPLEYBY	WLM 556	SCIOTO	WLR 65504
FRANK DREW	WLM 557	OSAGE	WLR 65505
ANTHONY PETIT	WLM 558	SANGAMON	WLR 65506
BARBARA MARBRITY	WLM 559	WEDGE	WLR 75307

Ship	Hull Number	Ship	Hull Number
GASCONADE	WLR 75401	**Harbour Tugs Small**	
MUSKINGUM	WLR 75402		
WYACONDA	WLR 75403	CAPSTAN	WYTL 65601
CHIPPEWA	WLR 75404	CHOCK	WYTL 65602
CHEYENNE	WLR 75405	TACKLE	WYTL 65604
KICKAPOO	WLR 75406	BRIDLE	WYTL 65607
KANAWHA	WLR 75407	PENDANT	WYTL 65608
PATOKA	WLR 75408	SHACKLE	WYTL 65609
CHENA	WLR 75409	HAWSER	WYTL 65610
KANKAKEE	WLR 75500	LINE	WYTL 65611
GREENBRIER	WLR 75501	WIRE	WYTL 65612
		BOLLARD	WYTL 65614
Icebreaking Tugs		CLEAT	WYTL 65615
KATMAI BAY	WTGB 101		
BRISTOL BAY	WTGB 102		
MOBILE BAY	WTGB 103		
BISCAYNE BAY	WTGB 104		
NEAH BAY	WTGB 105		
MORRO BAY	WTGB 106		
PENOBSCOT BAY	WTGB 107		
THUNDER BAY	WTGB 108		
STURGEON BAY	WTGB 109		

USCGC Polar Star

ICEBREAKERS
POLAR CLASS

Ship	Hull Number	Completion Date	Builder
POLAR STAR	10	1976	Lockheed SB

Machinery: CODOG; diesel-electric; 6 Alco 16V-251F/ Westinghouse AC diesel generators, 21,000 hp; 3 Westinghouse DC motors 18,000 hp; 3 Pratt & Whitney FT4A-12 gas turbines; 3 shafts **Displacement:** 13,190 tons **Dimensions:** 121.6m x 25.6m x 9.8m **Speed:** 20 knots **Armament:** 2 x 7.62 MG **Aircraft:** 2 x HH-65A or 1 x HH-60J **Complement:** 134 plus 33 scientists and 12 aircrew.

Notes: This ship is specifically designed for open ocean ice breaking and is fitted with reinforced hulls and bows that enable it to cut through pack ice. A special ballast system installed aboard allows the ship to shift its position to help smash through the ice. The ship conducts operations in both the Arctic and Antarctic regions and based at Seattle. POLAR STAR received a three year refit between 2010 and 2013.

Sister ship POLAR SEA has been alongside at Seattle and has been progressively stripped of parts to keep her sister ship operational.

USCGC Healy

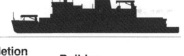

HEALY CLASS

Ship	Hull Number	Completion Date	Builder
HEALY	20	1999	Avondale

Machinery: Diesel-electric; 4 Westinghouse/Sulzer 12ZA 40S diesels; 42,400 hp; 4 Westinghouse alternators; 2 motors, 30,000 hp; 2 shafts; bow thruster **Displacement:** 16,663 tons FL **Dimensions:** 128m x 25m x 8.9m **Speed:** 17 knots **Aircraft:** 2 x HH-65A or 1 x HH-60J **Complement:** 75 (plus 45 scientists).

Notes: This icebreaker has the power to smash her way through 4.5 feet of ice at three knots continuously or up to eight feet thick ice by ramming. She has been designed to conduct a wide range of scientific and research activities and for this she is equipped with 4,200 square feet of scientific laboratory space and accommodation for up to 50 scientists.

On 5 September 2015, USCGC HEALY became the first unaccompanied United States surface vessel to reach the North Pole. With the age and increasing obsolescence of the Polar-class ships the United States Coast Guard continue to assess the requirements for future icebreakers.

USCGC Mackinaw

MACKINAW CLASS

Ship	Hull Number	Completion Date	Builder
MACKINAW	30	2006	Manitowoc Marine

Machinery: 3 Caterpillar 3612 Turbo-charged V-12 engines; 2 podded propulsors
Displacement: 3,500 tons **Dimensions:** 73.1m x 17.7m x 4.8m **Speed:** 15 knots
Complement: 55

Notes: MACKINAW is an icebreaker that can conduct heavy icebreaking duties and keeps the shipping lanes open on the Great Lakes. She is equipped with two 360 degree azimuthal propulsion pods and together with a powerful bow thruster the ship has an enhanced manoeuvrability capability. MACKINAW can break ice between 0.8 metres thick to 3.05 metres. When she was designed the Coast Guard took the opportunity to give the ship state-of-the-art multi mission capabilities that include search and rescue, buoy tending, maritime homeland security as well as law enforcement and environmental protection roles. She was commissioned on 10 June 2006 and is homeported at Cheboygan, Michigan.

USCG/PO3 MATTHEW WEST

USCGC Munro

MARITIME SECURITY CUTTER (LARGE)

Ship	Hull Number	Completion Date	Builder
BERTHOLF	750	2008	NG Ingalls Shipbuilding
WAESCHE	751	2009	NG Ingalls Shipbuilding
STRATTON	752	2011	NG Ingalls Shipbuilding
HAMILTON	753	2014	NG Ingalls Shipbuilding
JAMES	754	2015	NG Ingalls Shipbuilding
MUNRO	755	2017	NG Ingalls Shipbuilding
KIMBALL	756	2019	NG Ingalls Shipbuilding
MIDGETT	757	2019	NG Ingalls Shipbuilding
STONE	758	Building	NG Ingalls Shipbuilding
Unnamed	759	Contracted	NG Ingalls Shipbuilding
Unnamed	760	Contracted	NG Ingalls Shipbuilding

Machinery: CODAG: Two MTU-Detroit diesels (9,655 bhp); One GE LM2500 gas turbine (30,565 shp); two shafts **Displacement:** 4,500 tons (FL) **Dimensions:** 127.4m x 16.5m x 6.4m **Speed:** 28 knots **Armament:** 1 x 57mm; 1 x Vulcan Phalanx; 4 x 12.7mm MG **Complement:** 106 **Aircraft:** 1 x HH-65 Dolphin or 1 x HH-60J Jayhawk

Notes: Known as the Legend Class these ships are the future flagships of the US Coast Guard and have been designed to carry weaponry and systems suitable to perform their primary task of maritime security and national defence. Each ship has a stern ramp that enables the launch and recovery of their embarked small boats in higher sea states than was previously possible. These boats are also of a much newer and technologically advanced design with each ship carrying a Long-Range Interceptor and a Short-Range Prosecutor.

The Legend Class have a range of enhancements over previous US Coast Guard cutters including a larger flight deck, improved and more reliable machinery that gives better performance and increased range and enhanced weaponry. Inside the ships improved Command, Control and Communication aids reconnaissance and security missions.

USCG/CPO SARA MUIR   USCGC Kimball

USCGC Mellon

HIGH ENDURANCE CUTTER

Ship	Hull Number	Completion Date	Builder
MELLON	717	1967	Avondale Shipyards
MUNRO	724	1971	Avondale Shipyards
MIDGETT	726	1972	Avondale Shipyards

Machinery: CODOG; Two Pratt & Whitney FT4A-6 gas turbines 36,000 hp (27,000 kW); Two Fairbanks-Morse 38TD8-1/8-12 12-cylinder diesel engines 7,000 hp **Displacement:** 3,300 tons **Dimensions:** 115.2m x 13.1m x 6.1m **Speed:** 29 knots **Armament:** 1 x 76mm Oto Melara; 2 x 25mm Bushmaster; 1 x Vulcan Phalanx; 4 x 12.7mm MG **Complement:** 162 **Aircraft:** 1 x HH-65 Dolphin; HH-60J Jayhawk or MH-68A

Notes: These are the last surviving members of the Hamilton Class of High Endurance Cutters that made up the mainstay of the US Coast fleet from the 1970s to the early 2010s. Most of the class have now been sold abroad for further service whilst the American examples have been progressively replaced by the new Legend Class in service. This last trio of vessels will be sold for either foreign service or scrap in the next few years.

USCGC Tahoma

MEDIUM ENDURANCE CUTTER
FAMOUS CLASS

Ship	Hull Number	Completion Date	Builder
BEAR	901	1983	Tacoma Boatbuilding Co
TAMPA	902	1984	Tacoma Boatbuilding Co
HARRIET LANE	903	1984	Tacoma Boatbuilding Co
NORTHLAND	904	1984	Tacoma Boatbuilding Co
SPENCER	905	1986	Robert E Derecktor Corp
SENECA	906	1987	Robert E Derecktor Corp
ESCANABA	907	1987	Robert E Derecktor Corp
TAHOMA	908	1988	Robert E Derecktor Corp
CAMPBELL	909	1988	Robert E Derecktor Corp
THETIS	910	1989	Robert E Derecktor Corp
FORWARD	911	1990	Robert E Derecktor Corp
LEGARE	912	1990	Robert E Derecktor Corp
MOHAWK	913	1991	Robert E Derecktor Corp

Machinery: Two turbo-charged ALCO V-18 diesel engines driving two shafts with controllable pitch propellers **Displacement:** 1,820 tons **Dimensions:** 82.3m x 11.6m x 4.2m **Speed:** 19.5 knots **Armament:** 1 x 76mm Oto Melara; 2 x 12.7mm MG or 2 x 40mm Grenade Launchers; Mk 36 SRBOC decoy system **Complement:** 100 (plus 5 aircrew) **Aircraft:** 1 x HH-65 Dolphin; HH-60J Jayhawk; MH-68A or SH-60B.

Notes: These ships have undergone a Service Life Extension Program under the auspices of the Mission Effectiveness Project. Levels of habitability were improved as were the main machinery spaces. In order to keep these vessels operational well into the 2030s the US Coast Guard harvested weapons systems from decommissioned US Navy Oliver Hazard Perry-class frigates including Mk 75 76mm/62 calibre gun mounts, gun control panels, barrels, launchers and junction boxes and installed them aboard Famous-class vessels. This action saved the US Coast Guard around US$24 million.

USCG/PO2 ELISHA DAWKINS   USCGC Bear

USCGC Decisive

RELIANCE CLASS

Ship	Hull Number	Completion Date	Builder
RELIANCE	615	1964	Todd Shipyards
DILIGENCE	616	1964	Todd Shipyards
VIGILANT	617	1964	Todd Shipyards
ACTIVE	618	1966	Christy Corporation
CONFIDENCE	619	1966	Coast Guard Yard, Baltimore
RESOLUTE	620	1966	Coast Guard Yard, Baltimore
VALIANT	621	1967	American Shipbuilding Co
STEADFAST	623	1968	American Shipbuilding Co
DAUNTLESS	624	1968	American Shipbuilding Co
VENTUROUS	625	1968	American Shipbuilding Co
DEPENDABLE	626	1968	American Shipbuilding Co
VIGOROUS	627	1969	American Shipbuilding Co
DECISIVE	629	1968	Coast Guard Yard, Baltimore
ALERT	630	1969	Coast Guard Yard, Baltimore

Machinery: 2 Alco 16V-251 diesels 6,480 hp; driving 2 shafts **Displacement:** 1,129 tons **Dimensions:** 64.2m x 10.4m x 3.2m **Speed:** 18 knots **Armament:** 1 x 25mm Bushmaster; 2 x 12.7mm MG **Complement:** 75 **Aircraft:** 1 x HH-65 Dolphin or 1 x HH-60J Jayhawk.

Notes: These venerable vessels are primarily tasked with law enforcement and search and rescue missions within 500 nautical miles of the coastline. To facilitate this role the ships have excellent all-round vision from their specially designed bridge and a flight deck large enough to handle a medium sized helicopter. The class were given a life extension program that will see them through to the end of their extended careers. The new Heritage-class offshore patrol cutters will gradually replace these vessels in service.

USCGC Confidence

USCGC Alex Haley

EDENTON CLASS

Ship	Hull Number	Completion Date	Builder
ALEX HALEY	39	1971	Brooke Marine, Lowestoft

Machinery: Four Caterpillar 3516 DITAWJ diesels, 6,000 hp; 2 shafts **Displacement:** 3,000 tons **Dimensions:** 86.1m x 15.2m x 4.6m **Speed:** 18 knots **Armament:** 1 x 25mm Bushmaster; 2 x 12.7mm MG **Complement:** 99 **Aircraft:** Flightdeck for 1 x HH-65 Dolphin or 1 x HH-60J Jayhawk

Notes: Formerly a US Navy salvage vessel named USS EDENTON this vessel was subsequently transferred to the US Coast Guard and renamed as ALEX HALEY. During the conversion to US Coast Guard Cutter much of the former salvage gear was removed from the ship to allow for the installation of a flight deck, retractable hanger and new air search radar. She is used in the Bering Sea, Gulf of Alaska and Pacific regions.

USCGC Donald Horsley

SENTINEL CLASS

Ship	Hull Number	Completion Date	Builder
BERNARD C. WEBBER	1101	2012	Bollinger
RICHARD ETHERIDGE	1102	2012	Bollinger
WILLIAM FLORES	1103	2012	Bollinger
ROBERT YERED	1104	2013	Bollinger
MARGARET NORVELL	1105	2013	Bollinger
PAUL CLARK	1106	2013	Bollinger
CHARLES DAVID	1107	2013	Bollinger
CHARLES SEXTON	1108	2013	Bollinger
KATHLEEN MOORE	1109	2014	Bollinger
RAYMOND EVANS	1110	2014	Bollinger
WILLIAM TRUMP	1111	2015	Bollinger
ISAAC MAYO	1112	2015	Bollinger
RICHARD DIXON	1113	2015	Bollinger
HERIBERTO HERNANDEZ	1114	2015	Bollinger
JOSEPH NAPIER	1115	2016	Bollinger

Ship	Hull Number	Completion Date	Builder
WILLIAM GRIESSER	1116	2016	Bollinger
DONALD HORSLEY	1117	2016	Bollinger
JOSEPH TEZANOS	1118	2016	Bollinger
ROLLIN FRITCH	1119	2017	Bollinger
LAWRENCE LAWSON	1120	2017	Bollinger
JOHN McCORMICK	1121	2017	Bollinger
BAILEY BARCO	1122	2017	Bollinger
BENJAMIN DAILEY	1123	2017	Bollinger
OLIVER F. BERRY	1124	2017	Bollinger
JACOB POROO	1125	2018	Bollinger
JOSEPH GERCZAK	1126	2018	Bollinger
RICHARD SNYDER	1127	2018	Bollinger
NATHAN BRUCKENTHAL	1128	2018	Bollinger
FORREST O. REDNOUR	1129	2018	Bollinger
ROBERT G. WARD	1130	2019	Bollinger
TERRELL HORNE	1131	2019	Bollinger
BENJAMIN A. BOTTOMS	1132	2019	Bollinger
JOSEPH O. DOYLE	1133	2019	Bollinger
WILLIAM C. HART	1134	Building	Bollinger
ANGELA McSHAN	1135	Building	Bollinger
DANIEL TARR	1136	Building	Bollinger
EDGAR CULBERTSON	1137	Building	Bollinger
HAROLD MILLER	1138	Building	Bollinger
MYRTLE HAZARD	1139	Building	Bollinger
OLIVER HENRY	1140	Building	Bollinger
CHARLES MOULTROP	1141	Building	Bollinger
ROBERT GOLDMAN	1142	Building	Bollinger
FREDERICK HATCH	1143	Building	Bollinger
GLENN HARRIS	1144	Building	Bollinger
EMLEN TUNNELL	1145	Building	Bollinger

Ship	Hull Number	Completion Date	Builder
JOHN SCHEUERMAN	1146	Building	Bollinger
CLARENCE SUTPHIN	1147	Building	Bollinger
PABLO VALENT	1148	Building	Bollinger
DOUGLAS DENMAN	1149	Building	Bollinger
WILLIAM CHADWICK	1150	Building	Bollinger
WARREN DEYAMPERT	1151	Building	Bollinger
MAURICE JESTER	1152	Building	Bollinger
JOHN PATTERSON	1153	Building	Bollinger
WILLIAM SPARLING	1154	Building	Bollinger
Unnamed	1155	On order	Bollinger
Unnamed	1156	On order	Bollinger
Unnamed	1157	On order	Bollinger

Machinery: Two 20-cylinder MTU diesel engines; 2 shafts **Displacement:** 353 tons **Dimensions:** 46.8m x 8.11m x 2.9m **Speed:** 28 knots **Armament:** 25mm chain gun; four .50 calibre MG **Complement:** 22

Notes: In 2008 Bollinger Shipyard Inc was awarded the contract to design and build the first of a new class of cutter for the US Coast Guard to replace the ageing 110ft ocean going patrol boats. The design chosen was based on the Dutch Damen 4708 design modified to suit US Coast Guard requirements. The contract worth US$1.5 billion stipulated that up to 34 vessels. Further awards have subsequently raised that number with an expected total class numbering 58 vessels. Bollinger expects to deliver one vessel to the Coast Guard every eight weeks.

OFFSHORE PATROL CUTTER
HERITAGE CLASS

Ship	Hull Number	Comm Date	Builder
ARGUS	WMSM-915	On order	Eastern Shipbuilding, Florida
CHASE	WMSM-916	On order	Eastern Shipbuilding, Florida
INGHAM	WMSM-917	Projected	Eastern Shipbuilding, Florida
RUSH	WMSM-918	Projected	Eastern Shipbuilding, Florida
PICKERING	WMSM-919	Projected	Eastern Shipbuilding, Florida
ICARUS	WMSM-920	Projected	Eastern Shipbuilding, Florida
ACTIVE	WMSM-921	Projected	Eastern Shipbuilding, Florida
DILIGENCE	WMSM-922	Projected	Eastern Shipbuilding, Florida
ALERT	WMSM-923	Projected	Eastern Shipbuilding, Florida
VIGILANT	WMSM-924	Projected	Eastern Shipbuilding, Florida
RELIANCE	WMSM-925	Projected	Eastern Shipbuilding, Florida

Machinery: 2 x 7,280 kW (9,760hp) MAN 16V28/33D STC diesel engines **Displacement:** 3,730 tons FL **Dimensions:** 110m x 16m x 5.2m **Speed:** 22+ knots **Endurance:** 6o days **Armament:** 1 x Bofors Mk110 57mm gun; 1 x BAE Mk 38 Mod 2

25mm gun; 2 x Browning .50 cal (12.7mm) MG on remote controlled Small Arms Mount; 2 x Mk2 Browning MG **Aircraft:** 1 x MH-60 or MH65 plus UAS **Complement:** 126

Notes: This new design will, eventually, replace the existing legacy cutters of the Reliance and Sentinel Classes in service and will perform the whole range of Coast Guard missions including, but not exclusively, Maritime Law Enforcement, search and rescue, environmental protection and drug/migrant interdiction. The class has been designed to offer better levels of combat survivability and will be fitted with armour plating over vital areas. Interoperability with US Navy and foreign assets was a key factor in the design. Another key aspect of the Heritage Class is the installation of the Saab Sea Giraffe AN/SPS-77 multi-mode medium range naval radar system which provides the ship with enhanced 3D air and surface search functions.

In September 2016, the US$110.3 million contract to build the first of class was awarded to Eastern Shipbuilding of Panama City, Florida. It is expected that this class will, eventually, total some 25 vessels which will cost the US Coast Guard in the region of US$10.5 billion to build.

The first Heritage-class cutter, USCGC ARGUS, is expected to be accepted into service in August 2021.

USCGC Baranof

110' ISLAND CLASS

Ship	Hull Number	Completion Date	Builder
MAUI	1304	1986	Bollinger, Lockport
OCRACOKE	1307	1986	Bollinger, Lockport
AQUIDNECK	1309	1986	Bollinger, Lockport
MUSTANG	1310	1986	Bollinger, Lockport
NAUSHON	1311	1986	Bollinger, Lockport
SANIBEL	1312	1987	Bollinger, Lockport
BARANOF	1318	1988	Bollinger, Lockport
CHANDELEUR	1319	1988	Bollinger, Lockport
CUTTYHUNK	1322	1988	Bollinger, Lockport
KEY LARGO	1324	1988	Bollinger, Lockport
MONOMOY	1326	1989	Bollinger, Lockport
SITKINAK	1329	1989	Bollinger, Lockport
TYBEE	1330	1989	Bollinger, Lockport
WASHINGTON	1331	1989	Bollinger, Lockport

Ship	Hull Number	Completion Date	Builder
WRANGELL	1332	1989	Bollinger, Lockport
ADAK	1333	1989	Bollinger, Lockport
LIBERTY	1334	1989	Bollinger, Lockport
ANACAPA	1335	1989	Bollinger, Lockport
KISKA	1336	1989	Bollinger, Lockport

Machinery: Two Caterpillar 3516 DITA diesels (A &B series); 2 shafts **Displacement:** 168 tons (A series); 154 tons (B series) **Dimensions:** 33.5m x 6.4m x 2.2m **Speed:** 29 knots **Armament:** 1 x 25mm; 2 x 12.7mm MG **Complement:** 16

Notes: This class was based on the Vosper Thornycroft 110ft patrol boat design and has served the US Coast well for the last four decades. They were acquired in three batches: A: 1301-1316, B: 1317-1337 and C: 1338-1349. They are now nearing the end of their service careers and are being gradually replaced by newer Sentinel Class vessels. Many of the class are forward deployed to the Gulf or Japan.

USCGC Sea Dog (front) and USCGC Sea Dragon

87' MARINE PROTECTOR CLASS

Ship	Hull Number	Completion Date	Builder
BARRACUDA	87301	1998	Bollinger, Lockport
HAMMERHEAD	87302	1998	Bollinger, Lockport
MAKO	87303	1998	Bollinger, Lockport
MARLIN	87304	1998	Bollinger, Lockport
STINGRAY	87305	1999	Bollinger, Lockport
DORADO	87306	1999	Bollinger, Lockport
OSPREY	87307	1999	Bollinger, Lockport
CHINOOK	87308	1999	Bollinger, Lockport
ALBACORE	87309	1999	Bollinger, Lockport
TARPON	87310	1999	Bollinger, Lockport
COBIA	87311	1999	Bollinger, Lockport
HAWKSBILL	87312	1999	Bollinger, Lockport
CORMORANT	87313	1999	Bollinger, Lockport
FINBACK	87314	1999	Bollinger, Lockport

Ship	Hull Number	Completion Date	Builder
AMBERJACK	87315	1999	Bollinger, Lockport
KITTIWAKE	87316	2000	Bollinger, Lockport
BLACKFIN	87317	2000	Bollinger, Lockport
BLUEFIN	87318	2000	Bollinger, Lockport
YELLOWFIN	87319	2000	Bollinger, Lockport
MANTA	87320	2000	Bollinger, Lockport
COHO	87321	2000	Bollinger, Lockport
KINGFISHER	87322	2000	Bollinger, Lockport
SEAHAWK	87323	2000	Bollinger, Lockport
STEELHEAD	87324	2000	Bollinger, Lockport
BELUGA	87325	2000	Bollinger, Lockport
BLACKTIP	87326	2000	Bollinger, Lockport
PELICAN	87327	2000	Bollinger, Lockport
RIDLEY	87328	2000	Bollinger, Lockport
COCHITO	87329	2001	Bollinger, Lockport
MANOWAR	87330	2001	Bollinger, Lockport
MORAY	87331	2001	Bollinger, Lockport
RAZORBILL	87332	2001	Bollinger, Lockport
ADELIE	87333	2001	Bollinger, Lockport
GANNET	87334	2001	Bollinger, Lockport
NARWHAL	87335	2001	Bollinger, Lockport
STURGEON	87336	2001	Bollinger, Lockport
SOCKEYE	87337	2001	Bollinger, Lockport
IBIS	87338	2001	Bollinger, Lockport
POMPANO	87339	2001	Bollinger, Lockport
HALIBUT	87340	2001	Bollinger, Lockport
BONITO	87341	2001	Bollinger, Lockport
SHRIKE	87342	2002	Bollinger, Lockport
TERN	87343	2002	Bollinger, Lockport

Ship	Hull Number	Completion Date	Builder
HERON	87344	2002	Bollinger, Lockport
WAHOO	87345	2002	Bollinger, Lockport
FLYING FISH	87346	2002	Bollinger, Lockport
HADDOCK	87347	2002	Bollinger, Lockport
BRANT	87348	2002	Bollinger, Lockport
SHEARWATER	87349	2002	Bollinger, Lockport
PETREL	87350	2002	Bollinger, Lockport
SEALION	87352	2003	Bollinger, Lockport
SKIPJACK	87353	2003	Bollinger, Lockport
DOLPHIN	87354	2004	Bollinger, Lockport
HAWK	87355	2004	Bollinger, Lockport
SAILFISH	87356	2004	Bollinger, Lockport
SAWFISH	87357	2004	Bollinger, Lockport
SWORDFISH	87358	2005	Bollinger, Lockport
TIGER SHARK	87359	2005	Bollinger, Lockport
BLUE SHARK	87360	2005	Bollinger, Lockport
SEA HORSE	87361	2005	Bollinger, Lockport
SEA OTTER	87362	2005	Bollinger, Lockport
MANATEE	87363	2005	Bollinger, Lockport
AHI	87364	2006	Bollinger, Lockport
PIKE	87365	2006	Bollinger, Lockport
TERRAPIN	87366	2006	Bollinger, Lockport
SEA DRAGON	87367	2008	Bollinger, Lockport
SEA DEVIL	87368	2008	Bollinger, Lockport
CROCODILE	87369	2008	Bollinger, Lockport
DIAMONDBACK	87370	2008	Bollinger, Lockport
REEF SHARK	87371	2008	Bollinger, Lockport
ALLIGATOR	87372	2009	Bollinger, Lockport
SEA DOG	87373	2009	Bollinger, Lockport
SEA FOX	87374	2009	Bollinger, Lockport

Machinery: Two MTU 8V 396 TE94 diesels; 2 shafts **Displacement:** 91 tons
Dimensions: 26.5m x 5.8m x 1.6m **Speed:** 25 knots **Armament:** 2 x 12.7mm MG
Complement: 10

Notes: This class was designed to operate in the littoral region between the coastline and the deeper oceans and has proved to be a highly successful design. The main roles these craft are put to are search and rescue, law enforcement, fisheries, drug interdiction and alien interdiction. In the last two decades they have also assumed a much more aggressive role in pursuance of Homeland Security missions.

SEA DRAGON, SEA DEVIL, SEA DOG and SEA FOX were bought by the US Navy and are operated by the US Coast Guard. They have the specialist role of protecting and escorting US Navy submarines, especially the Ohio-class ballistic missile submarines, at their bases at Banger, Maine and Kings Bay. For this role these four vessels are fitted with a remote controlled .50 calibre mount on a raised platform on the forecastle.

A smaller class of a dozen 64 foot long 'Screening Escort Vessels' are owned by the US Navy but operated by the US Coast Guard and feature waterjet propulsion. They are employed for naval asset protection duties as well as for search and rescue missions.

USCG/PO3 DAVID MARIN

USCGC Shearwater

USCGC Eagle

SAIL TRAINING SHIP

Ship	Hull Number	Completion Date	Builder
EAGLE	WIX-327	1936	Blohm & Voss

Machinery: One Caterpillar D399 auxiliary diesel; 1 shaft **Displacement:** 1,816 tons **Dimensions:** 70.4/89.5m x 12m x 4.9m **Sail Area:** 25,351 ft **Speed:** 10.5 knots (18 under sail) **Complement:** 12 Officers; 38 Crew; 150 Cadets

Notes: EAGLE is a three masted sailing barque built in Nazi Germany by Blohm and Voss shipbuilders at Hamburg as a sail training vessel for the German Kriegsmarine. She was originally commissioned as the HORST WESSEL and following the end of World War Two was passed to the United States as war reparations. She was renamed EAGLE and on May 15, 1946 she was commissioned into service and sailed for her new home in America. She serves as a seagoing training vessel for Coast Guard Cadets with classrooms onboard able to accommodate 175 cadets and instructors. When not sailing she is based at the Coast Guard Academy on the Thames River.

USCGC Cypress

SEAGOING BUOY TENDERS
JUNIPER CLASS

Ship	Hull Number	Completion Date	Builder
JUNIPER	201	1996	Marinette Marine
WILLOW	202	1996	Marinette Marine
KUKUI	203	1997	Marinette Marine
ELM	204	1998	Marinette Marine
WALNUT	205	1999	Marinette Marine
SPAR	206	2001	Marinette Marine
MAPLE	207	2001	Marinette Marine
ASPEN	208	2001	Marinette Marine
SYCAMORE	209	2002	Marinette Marine
CYPRESS	210	2002	Marinette Marine
OAK	211	2002	Marinette Marine
HICKORY	212	2003	Marinette Marine
FIR	213	2003	Marinette Marine

Ship	Hull Number	Completion Date	Builder
HOLLYHOCK	214	2003	Marinette Marine
SEQUOIA	215	2004	Marinette Marine
ALDER	216	2004	Marinette Marine

Machinery: Two Caterpillar 3608 diesels; 1 shaft, 3,100 hp **Displacement:** 2,064 tons FL **Dimensions:** 68.6m x 14m x 4m **Speed:** 16 knots **Armament:** Provision for 1 x Mk 38 25 mm naval gun and 2 x .50 caliber MG **Complement:** 8 officers and 40 enlisted

Notes: This class of buoy tenders replaced an older selection of vessels and introduced new levels of sophistication and technology to the task. The ships were built by Marinette Marine and are equipped with a single controllable pitch propeller, bow and stern thrusters which are linked closely to a global positioning system that allows the ships to be manoeuvred to exactly the right spot with precision. The Juniper Class also boasts the ability to break ice up to 14 inches thick at 3 knots or 3ft thick by ramming it. They also have a limited salvage and oil spill capability.

USCGC James Rankin

COASTAL BUOY TENDERS
KEEPER CLASS

Ship	Hull Number	Completion Date	Builder
IDA LEWIS	551	1996	Marinette Marine
KATHERINE WALKER	552	1997	Marinette Marine
ABBIE BURGESS	553	1997	Marinette Marine
MARCUS HANNA	554	1997	Marinette Marine
JAMES RANKIN	555	1998	Marinette Marine
JOSHUA APPLEYBY	556	1998	Marinette Marine
FRANK DREW	557	1998	Marinette Marine
ANTHONY PETIT	558	1999	Marinette Marine
BARBARA MARBRITY	559	1999	Marinette Marine
WILLIAM TATE	560	1999	Marinette Marine
HARRY CLAIBORNE	561	1999	Marinette Marine
MARIA BRAY	562	2000	Marinette Marine
HENRY BLAKE	563	2000	Marinette Marine
GEORGE COBB	564	2000	Marinette Marine

Machinery: Two Caterpillar 3508TA diesels; 2 Ulstein Z-drives; bow thruster
Displacement: 840 tons FL **Dimensions:** 53.3m x 11m x 2.4m **Speed:** 12 knots
Complement: 18

Notes: These vessels are utilised for the maintenance of navigational aids around the
US coastline. Additionally, they can be tasked with search and rescue, drug and alien
interdiction, environmental control and natural resources management. Keeper-class
vessels have a limited ice breaking ability. They are fitted with sophisticated manoeuvring
thrusters that allow each vessel to position themselves extremely precisely.

● USCG/PO3 Jonathan Klingenberg   **USCG Bluebell**

INLAND BUOY TENDERS

Ship	Hull Number	Comm Date	Builder
BLUEBELL	313	1944	Birchfield Boiler Co.
BUCKTHORN	642	1963	Mobile Ship Repair

Machinery: Two Caterpillar diesels; 2 shafts **Displacement:** 226 tons, 174 tons
(BLUEBELL) **Dimensions:** 30.5m x 7.3m x 1.5m (BUCKTHORN draft 1.2m) **Speed:**
11.9 knots **Complement:** 15

Notes: Two vessels from different eras but performing the same task that of maintaining
inland navigational aids and buoys. BLUEBELL is based at Portland, Oregon whilst
BUCKTHORN is based at Sault Sainte Marie in Mississippi.

INLAND BUOY TENDERS
BAYBERRY CLASS

Ship	Hull Number	Completion Date	Builder
BAYBERRY	65400	1954	Reliable Shipyard, Olympia
ELDERBERRY	65401	1954	Reliable Shipyard, Olympia

Machinery: Two GM diesels; 2 shafts **Displacement:** 70 tons FL **Dimensions:** 19.8m x 5.2m x 1.2m **Speed:** 10 knots **Complement:** 8

Notes: Two elderly vessels responsible for the upkeep of navigational buoys on inland waterways. BAYBERRY is based at Seattle and ELDERBERRY is based at Petersburg, Alaska.

CONSTRUCTION TENDERS
PAMLICO CLASS

Ship	Hull Number	Completion Date	Builder
PAMLICO	800	1976	CG Yard, Curtis Bay Md
HUDSON	801	1976	CG Yard, Curtis Bay Md
KENNEBEC	802	1977	CG Yard, Curtis Bay Md
SAGINAW	803	1977	CG Yard, Curtis Bay Md

Machinery: Two Caterpillar diesels; 2 shafts **Displacement:** 416 tons **Dimensions:** 48.8m x 9.1m x 1.2m **Speed:** 10 knots **Complement:** 14

Notes: These tenders share many roles with other Coast Guard cutters but have a specially extended forecastle on which construction equipment such as cranes can be positioned to better aid the installation and maintenance of navigational aids and buoys. HUDSON is based at Miami Beach, Florida; KENNEBEC at Portsmouth, Virginia; PAMLICO is based at New Orleans whilst SAGINAW is at Mobile, Alabama.

COSMOS CLASS

Ship	Hull Number	Completion Date	Builder
SMILAX	315	1944	Dubuque Boat & Boiler

Machinery: Diesel; 600 shp; 2 shafts **Displacement:** 178 tons **Dimensions:** 30.5m x 7.3m x 1.5m **Speed:** 10.5 knots **Complement:** 14

Notes: This vessel was constructed during the Second World War and is still in active service making her the oldest ship in the US Coast Guard fleet and is honoured as such by being affectionately given the title of Queen of the Fleet and allowed to display her hull numbers in gold. Her role in the fleet is as a construction barge, she is based at Atlantic Beach, North Carolina.

ANVIL CLASS

Ship	Hull Number	Comm Date	Builder
ANVIL	75301	1962	Gibbs Corporation, Jacksonville
HAMMER	75302	1962	Gibbs Corporation, Jacksonville
SLEDGE	75303	1962	McDermott Fabricators, Morgan City
MALLET	75304	1963	McDermott Fabricators, Morgan City
VISE	75305	1963	McDermott Fabricators, Morgan City
CLAMP	75306	1964	Sturgeon Bay SB & DD, Wisconsin
WEDGE	75307	1964	Sturgeon Bay SB & DD, Wisconsin
HATCHET	75309	1966	Dorchester SB, New Jersey
AXE	75310	1966	Dorchester SB, New Jersey

Machinery: Two Caterpillar diesels; 2 shafts **Displacement:** 140 tons **Dimensions:** 22.9m x 6.7m x 1.2m **Speed:** 10 knots **Complement:** 13

Notes: CLAMP, HATCHET and AXE are one foot longer than the rest of the class. These vessels can push both 68 foot and 84 foot construction barges. WEDGE is operated as River Tender (WLR).

USCGC Kanawha

RIVER TENDERS
GASCONADE CLASS

Ship	Hull Number	Completion Date	Builder
GASCONADE	75401	1964	St Louis SB & DD
MUSKINGUM	75402	1965	Maxon Construction Co
WYACONDA	75403	1965	Maxon Construction Co
CHIPPEWA	75404	1965	Maxon Construction Co
CHEYENNE	75405	1966	Maxon Construction Co
KICKAPOO	75406	1969	Halter Marine, New Orleans
KANAWHA	75407	1969	Halter Marine, New Orleans
PATOKA	75408	1970	Halter Marine, New Orleans
CHENA	75409	1970	Halter Marine, New Orleans
KANKAKEE	75500	1990	Avondale Industries
GREENBRIER	75501	1990	Avondale Industries

Machinery: Two Caterpillar diesels; 2 shafts **Displacement:** 150 tons **Dimensions:** 22.9m x 6.7m x 7m **Speed:** 9 knots **Complement:** 13

Notes: Aids to Navigation (ATON) is the Government Policy to maintain river navigation across the United States. These vessels are specially designed with flat bottoms and flat ends to allow them to navigate most navigable rivers across the country and are equipped with cranes and other equipment to lift, repair and replace navigational aids. KANKAKEE and GREENBRIER were approved in 1986 and ordered two years later. They act as push tugs for barges 74 and 75.

• USCG/LEN SCHULTE   **USCGC Sangamon**

OUACHITA CLASS

Ship	Hull Number	Completion Date	Builder
OUACHITA	65501	1960	Platzer SY Houston
CIMARRON	65502	1960	Platzer SY Houston
OBION	65503	1962	Gibbs Corp Jacksonville
SCIOTO	65504	1962	Gibbs Corp Jacksonville
OSAGE	65505	1962	Gibbs Corp Jacksonville
SANGAMON	65506	1962	Gibbs Corp Jacksonville

Machinery: Two Caterpillar diesels; 2 shafts **Displacement:** 146 tons **Dimensions:** 19.8m x 6.4m x 0.4m **Speed:** 10 knots **Complement:** 13

Notes: All these vessels are to be found operating on the Mississippi River and its tributaries and all have a 3 tons crane.

USCGC Katmai Bay

ICEBREAKING TUGS
BAY CLASS

Ship	Hull Number	Commission Date	Builder
KATMAI BAY	101	1979	Tacoma Boatbuilding
BRISTOL BAY	102	1979	Tacoma Boatbuilding
MOBILE BAY	103	1979	Tacoma Boatbuilding
BISCAYNE BAY	104	1979	Tacoma Boatbuilding
NEAH BAY	105	1980	Tacoma Boatbuilding
MORRO BAY	106	1981	Tacoma Boatbuilding
PENOBSCOT BAY	107	1984	Bay City Marine
THUNDER BAY	108	1985	Bay City Marine
STURGEON BAY	109	1988	Bay City Marine

Machinery: Diesel-Electric; 2 Fairbanks-Morse DG; 2 Westinghouse electric drive; 1 shaft **Displacement:** 662 tons **Dimensions:** 42.7m x 11.4m x 3.8m **Speed:** 14.7 knots **Complement:** 17

Notes: Strengthened tugs used primarily for domestic ice breaking duties and are mostly found operating around the Great Lakes or Northeast US areas. The tugs are fitted with a special low-pressure air bubbler system that reduces the resistance between the hull and the ice to break through. BRISTOL BAY and MOBILE BAY are augmented by a 120ft work barge for work with the maintenance of navigational aids.

USCGC Hawser

HARBOUR TUGS SMALL
CAPSTAN CLASS

Ship	Hull Number	Comm Date	Builder
CAPSTAN	65601	1961	Gibbs Corporation Jacksonville
CHOCK	65602	1962	Gibbs Corporation Jacksonville
TACKLE	65604	1962	Gibbs Corporation Jacksonville
BRIDLE	65607	1963	Barbour Boat, New Bern. NC
PENDANT	65608	1963	Barbour Boat, New Bern. NC
SHACKLE	65609	1963	Barbour Boat, New Bern. NC
HAWSER	65610	1963	Barbour Boat, New Bern. NC
LINE	65611	1963	Barbour Boat, New Bern. NC
WIRE	65612	1963	Barbour Boat, New Bern. NC
BOLLARD	65614	1967	Western Boat Building Corp
CLEAT	65615	1967	Western Boat Building Corp

Machinery: One Caterpillar 3412TA diesel; one shaft **Displacement:** 72 tons
Dimensions: 19.8m x 8.5m x 2.1m **Speed:** 10 knots **Complement:** 6

Notes: These tugs operate along the East Coast of the United States from Maine to Virginia and are routinely utilised in a wide variety of tasks including domestic ice operations, search and rescue, law enforcement and harbour duties.

47' MOTOR LIFE BOAT (MLB)

117 47-foot MLBs are currently in service throughout the United States. These vessels were built by Textron and provide a fast response rescue resource. The lifeboats are constructed from aluminium and are capable of withstanding some of the worst sea conditions imaginable. They are designed to be self-bailing and self-righting making the lifeboats virtually unsinkable. The boats are capable of maintaining 20 knots in 2-foot seas and are powered by a pair of Detroit 6V92 TA diesels.

45' RESPONSE BOAT MEDIUM (RB-M)

The first 45' Response Boat Medium was delivered from its manufactures to Little Creek in April 2008 and since then 174 have been handed over to the US Coast Guard. The RB-M conducts a range of vital missions including homeland security, search and rescue and law enforcement out to a distance of 50 nautical miles from shore. The boats are made from aluminium and boasts waterjet propulsion. Weapons can be mounted on fore and aft mounts when required.

35' LONG RANGE INTERCEPTOR (LRI)

This class of vessel is designed to be carried by the Bertholf-class cutters with each cutter able to accommodate up to three of the craft. The LRIs are fitted with radar and data links allowing them to extend the range and capabilities of the mother ship to well over the horizon.

The first example was built and displayed by Willard Marine in 2008. This prototype was not pursued and a larger more capable Mk II version of the design was instigated. The LR-II featured increased passenger capacity, improved hydrodynamic stability, higher speeds, ballistic protection and a hull design to allow retrieval by Coast Guard cutters.

A second vessel type, the Over the Horizon IV (OTH-IV) boat is also operated by the Bertholf Class and is being built by SAFE Boats International LLC of Port Orchard, Washington. Each is 26ft long and can operate at ranges of 200 nautical miles and speeds of 40 knots.

29' RESPONSE BOAT SMALL II (RB-S II)

Built by Metal Shark Aluminium Boats these small coastal craft are amongst the most numerous in the Coast Guard fleet. With an expected total of 500 examples the vessels are used for coastal work including search and rescue, law enforcement and surveillance duties.

The vessels can mount machine guns on fore and aft gun mounts and there is ballistic protection around the cabin. Each boat has a crew of four, a range of 150 nautical miles and a top speed of 45+ knots.

25' DEFENDER CLASS (RB-HS/RB-S)

Following the terrorist attacks on the World Trade Center in September 2001 an examination of contingencies found that there was a lack of small, highly agile and responsive waterborne craft in the US Coast Guard inventory. This study concluded that the purchase of the Defender Class was imperative and an emergency acquisition program was instigated. 500 standard response boats were ordered (470 for the US Coast Guard, 20 for the Department of Homeland Security and 10 for the US Navy).

In May 2002 the first of 100 Defender A Class were delivered with a follow on B Class starting from October 2003 and featuring a longer cabin and shock mounted seats for the crew. The Defenders are allocated to the Coast Guard's Maritime Safety and Security Teams (MSST), Maritime Security Response Team (MRST), Marine Safety Units (MSU) and Small Boat Stations throughout the Coast Guard.

The USCG also operates 52 Special Purpose Craft-Law Enforcement. These 33 foot long craft were built by SAFE Boats and are similar to the Defender Class and were delivered between 2006 and 2009.

21-64' AID TO NAVIGATION BOATS

The US Coast Guard operates a fleet of approximately 140 Aids to Navigation Boats of varying sizes, capabilities and ages and too numerous to list individually in a book of this size.

The majority of these vessels range in size from 21-64 feet in length and are designed to operate within the inland waters of the United States. Some, notably the 55' ANB are often employed to service offshore aids in addition to those inland. The 55' ANB is equipped with a crane used to hoisting and securing buoys and signal aids.

TRANSPORTABLE PORT SECURITY BOAT (TPSB)

One of the smallest vessels in the US Coast fleet yet some of the most capable at the same time, the Transportable Port Security Boat is 25 feet in length and powered by a twin outboard motor. Based on the tried and tested Boston Whaler design these small craft can be fitted with three machine guns positions fore and aft and can operate effectively in inner harbour or near shore environments. The first boat was built by Boston Whaler in Edgewater, Florida in 1997, since then over 50 vessels of this type have been delivered, with the majority being constructed by Kvichak Marine Industries, Inc of Seattle.

Finally, in addition to those already mentioned the US Coast Guard operates over 2,000 small craft ranging from screening vessels to multi-terrain Airboat Rescue Launches as well as numerous RIBs operated from various classes of cutter.

US COAST GUARD AVIATION

In its role of protecting the United States the US Coast Guard employs a variety of aerial platforms both from vessels at sea and from 18 land-based airfields across Continental US, Puerto Rico, Hawaii and Alaska.

The US Coast Guard owns over 200 aircraft which fluctuates according to availability based on maintenance schedules. The core missions of Coast Guard Aviation directly mirror those of the ship fleet namely Search and Rescue, Law Enforcement, Environmental Response, Ice Operations, and Air Interdiction.

Fixed wing operations utilise the C-130 Hercules and the HC-144A Ocean Sentry aircraft, whilst rotary wing operations with the H-65 Dolphin and the HH-60-Jayhawks can be from air capable cutters, Air Stations and Air Facilities.

Many of the Coast Guard's aircraft are reasonably old and replacement programs are at an advanced stage; but remain to be authorised in most cases. The US Coast Guard has suffered a problem with their fleet of older C-130 Hercules following a fatal crash in Alaska. The fleet was grounded whilst a solution was found that required many months of inactivity. New J model Hercules are on order from Lockheed and have been starting to make their presence felt in the fleet.

EADS/CASA HC-144A OCEAN SENTRY

Variants: HC-144A
Role: Medium Range Surveillance aircraft
Engines: Two General Electric CT7-93C Turboprop engines.
Length: 21.4 metres **Height:** 8.18 metres **Wingspan:** 25.81 metres
Speed: 246 knots **Ceiling:** 30,000+ feet **Range:** 2,000 nautical miles
Crew: 2 (minimum) **Endurance:** 11.5 hours

Notes: These aircraft provide homeland security missions in addition to their role as search and rescue, law enforcement, drug interdiction, environmental protection, international ice patrol and cargo and personnel transport missions. The Ocean Sentry is a highly capable and adaptable aircraft that has been upgraded with the addition of a Rockwell Collins Flight 2 glass cockpit instrument panel. Each of the 18 Ocean Sentrys in the US Coast Guard fleet is capable of embarking a mission specific equipment pallet. In this role the HC-144A has replaced the HU-25 Guardian and some HC-130 Hercules in the medium range surveillance and transport role. Originally the Coast Guard had wanted to purchase 36 aircraft but the offer of purchasing14 off the shelf and cheaper former US Air Force C-27J Spartan aircraft saw this program end at 18.

Lockheed HC-130 HERCULES

Variants: HC-130H; HC-130J
Role: Long Range Surveillance Aircraft
Engines: Four Allison T56-A15 turboprop engines (Allison AE2100D3 in HC-130J).
Length: 29.8 metres **Height:** 11.6 metres **Wingspan:** 40.4 metres
Speed: 330 knots (374 knots HC-130J) **Ceiling:** 33,000+ feet
Range: 4,100 nautical miles (5,000 nautical miles HC-130J).
Crew: 7
Endurance: 14 hours (21 hours HC-130J)

Notes: HC-130H Hercules transport aircraft are operated by the US Coast Guard from the five main Coast Guard air bases at CGAS Sacremento in California, CGAS Clearwater in Florida, CGAS Kodiak, Alaska and from CGAS Barbers Point in Hawaii. Nine of the newer, longer range HC-130Js operate from CGAS Elizabeth City in North Carolina. The HC-130J Hercules has been derived from the KC-130J tanker employed by the US Marine Corps. Amongst the numerous changes in design are the installation of an inverse synthetic aperture sea search radar, flare tubes, FLIR and large windows on each side of the fuselage to aid crew members visual searching of the sea surface. The first of the type was delivered to the US Coast Guard in October 2003. Seven former US Coast Guard HC-130Hs have been transferred to the US Forest Service. New aircraft are being delivered regularly to the US Coast Guard which expects all older H models to be replaced by J examples by 2027.

Gulfstream C-37A GULFSTREAM V

Variants: C-37A
Role: Command and Control Aircraft
Engines: Two 14,750 lb BMW-Rolls-Royce BR710-48 turbofans
Length: 29.4 metres **Height:** 7.87 metres **Wingspan:** 28.5 metres
Speed: 459 knots **Ceiling:** 54,000 feet **Range:** 5,500 nautical miles
Crew: 4

Notes: Two long range Gulfstream V aircraft are operated by the US Coast Guard as its principal Command and Control transport for travel by the Secretary of Homeland Security, the Coast Guard Commandant, and other US Officials. Twelve passengers are seated in comfort at high subsonic speeds. The two aircraft are referred to as CG-01 and CG-02 and based at Washington National Airport, Washington DC.

Eurocopter H-65 DOLPHIN

Variants: H-65B; H-65C; MH-65C
Role: Short Range Recovery Helicopter
Engines: Two Turbomeca Arriel 2C2-CG turboshaft engines
Length: 11.6 metres **Height:** 4.0 metres **Rotor Diameter:** 11.9 metres
Speed: 165 knots. **Ceiling:** 15,000 feet **Range:** 350 - 410 nautical miles.
Crew: 2 pilots and 2 crew.
Armament: One M240G 7.62mm MG and one Barrett M107CQ .50cal precision rifle
(MH-65C)

Notes: In 1979 the US Coast Guard selected the European SA 366 G1 Dauphin as its new short-range Recovery Helicopter over stiff domestic competition. To compensate for buying a foreign design, Aerospatiale of France established a factory in Grand Prairie, Texas to build the initial 99 aircraft to be acquired. Over the years new aircraft have been added bringing the total to 102 as of the time of writing this book. Furthermore, the aircraft have been upgraded on numerous occasions most notably in 2004 when they were retrofitted with new avionics with the resultant helicopters being reclassified as H-65C and MH-65Cs. In January 2011 the first MH-65D was completed and features enhanced avionics over the C variant including Honeywell HC7502 radar altimeter and two Honeywell H-764G EGIs (embedded GPS/inertial navigation system). 97 HH/MH-65Cs are in the process of being upgraded to D standard. A further upgrade adds the MH-65E to the fleet and will see those aircraft given the Common Avionics Architecture System (CAAS) installed in Coast Guard's upgraded MH-60T Jayhawk helicopters. The first MH-65E was delivered to the fleet in 2017.

Sikorsky HH-60J JAYHAWK

Variants: HH-60T
Role: Medium Range Recovery Helicopter
Engines: Two General Electric T700-401C gas turbines
Length: 19.76 metres **Height:** 5.18 metres **Rotor Diameter:** 16.36 metres
Speed: 180 knots **Ceiling:** 5,000 feet **Range:** 700 nautical miles.
Crew: 2 Pilots and two flight crew.
Armament: One 7.62 mm M240H medium MG in starboard door; One 12.7 mm
Barrett semi-automatic rifle

Notes: From 2007 the original HH-60J fleet was subjected to a retrofit program to equip the 42 helicopters for further service with the US Coast Guard. The refit saw the installation of superior avionics, a glass cockpit, an enhanced electro-optic/infrared sensor system as well as a radar sensor system and airborne use of force capability which includes both weapons for firing warning and disabling shots and armour to protect the aircrew from small arms fire. All 39 helicopters completed the upgrade program in February 2014, with three aircraft having been lost.

GLOSSARY

The military, throughout the world, have a passion for acronyms and abbreviations - and the US Armed Forces are no exception. Any modern day reference book will be liberally scattered with these, sometimes annoying, abbreviations - second nature to those in the know, but frustrating for the general reader. The following pages should help you through some of the 'alphabet soup' that will inevitably be found in this volume.

AAG	Advanced Arresting Gear	COMPTUEX	COMPosite Training Unit EXercise
ABM	Anti-Ballistic Missile		
AD	Destroyer Depot Ship	COMSEC	COMmunications SECurity
ADCAP	Advanced Capability	COTS	Commercial Off The Shelf
AEM/S	Advanced Enclosed Mast/Sensor	CRC	Coastal Riverine Company
		CRF	Coastal Riverine Force
AESA	Active Electronically Scanned Array	CSG	Carrier Strike Group
		CVBG	Carrier Battle Group
AFSB(I)	Afloat Forward Support Base (Interim)	CVN	Aircraft Carrier (Nuclear)
		CVW	Carrier Air Wing
AMDR	Air & Missile Defence Radar	DDG	Destroyer (Guided Missile)
ANB	Aids to Navigation Boats	DESDIV	DESstroyer DIVision
ARG	Amphibious Ready Group	DoD	Department of Defence
ARS	Auxiliary Rescue and Salvage Vessel	EFV	Expeditionary Fighting Vehicle
AS	Submarine Depot Ship	EMALS	Electro Magnetic Aircraft Launch System
ASROC	Anti-submarine Rocket		
ASUW	Anti-surface Warfare	EMNS	Expendable Mine Neutralization System
ASW	Anti-submarine Warfare		
ASWS	Auxiliary SeaWater System	ERO	Engineered Refueling Overhaul
ATON	Aids to Navigation		
BMD	Ballistic Missile Defence	ESG	Expeditionary Strike Group
CEC	Co-operative Engagement Capability	ESSM	Evolved Sea Sparrow Missile
C4ISR	Command, Control, Communications, Computers, Intelligence, Surveillance and Reconnaissance	EW	Electronic Warfare
		FADEC	Full Authority Digital Engine Control
		FDNF	Forward Deployed Naval Force
CG	Cruiser	FFG	Frigate (Guided Missile)
CG(X)	Cruiser (Next Generation)	FL	Full Load
CIVMAR	Civilian Mariner	FLIR	Forward Looking Infra-Red
CIWS	Close In Weapon System	FOD	Foreign Object Damage
CLF	Combat Logistics Force		(Debris and Detection also

	used in some cases)		Reconnaissance
FRC	Fast Response Cutter	JBD	Jet Blast Deflector (carriers)
FRP	Fleet Response Plan	JHSV	Joint High Speed Vessel
FSF	Fast Sea Frame	JPATS	Joint Primary Air Training
FSS	Fast Sealift Ship		System
FY	Financial Year	JTF	Joint Task Force
FYDP	Future Years Defence Plan	JTFEX	Joint Task Force Exercise
GTS	Gas Turbine Ship	LASH	Lighter Aboard Ship
GQ	General Quarters	LaWS	Laser Weapon System
	(Call to battle stations)	LCAC	Landing Craft (Air Cushion)
HELO	Helicopter	LCC	Amphibious Command
HM	Helicopter Mine Counter-		and Control Ship
	measures Squadron	LCS	Littoral Combat Ship
HMH	USMC Heavy Helicopter	LCU	Landing Craft (Utility)
	Squadron	LES	Leave and Earnings
HMLA	USMC Light Attack		Statement
	Helicopter Squadron	LFA	Low Frequency Array
HMM	USMC Medium Helicopter	LHA	Landing Ship, Helicopter
	Squadron		Assault
HMMT	USMC Heavy Helicopter	LHD	Landing Ship Helicopter,
	Training Squadron		Dock
HMT	USMC Helicopter Training	LMSR	Large, Medium Speed
	Squadron		Ro-Ro
HS	Helicopter ASW Squadron	LPD	Landing Ship, Personnel,
HSC	Helicopter Sea Combat		Dock
	Squadron	LRI	Long Range Interceptor
HSL	Helicopter ASW (Light)	LSD	Landing Ship, Dock
	Squadron	LST	Landing Ship, Tank
HSM	Helicopter Maritime Strike	LSV	Large Scale Vessel
	Squadron	MARAD	Maritime Administration
HST	High Speed Transport	MAW	USMC Air Wing
HSV	High Speed Vessel	MCAS	Marine Corps Air Station
HT	Helicopter Training	MCDS	Modular Cargo Delivery
	Squadron		System
HUQ	Unmanned Helicopter	MCM	Mine Countermeasures
	Squadron		Vessel
HX	Helicopter Trials Squadron	MCS	Mine Warfare Command
IBU	Inshore Boat Unit		and Support Vessel
ICBM	Inter Continental Ballistic	MDA	Missile Defence Agency
	Missile	MEF	Marine Expeditionary Force
ISR	Intelligence, Surveillance,	MG	Machine Gun

MHC	Coastal Minesweeper	NSC	National Security Cutter
MIRV	Multiple Independently	OPC	Offshore Patrol Cutter
	Targeted Re-entry Vehicles	OPDS	Offshore Petroleum
MLB	Motor Life Boat		Distribution System
MLE	Mission Life Extension	OPEVAL	Operational Evaluation
MMA	Multi-mission Maritime	PC	Patrol Craft
	Aircraft	PPIP	Planned Product
MMP	Multi-Mission Platform		Improvement Program
MPF	Maritime Pre-positioning	PRM	Pressurised Rescue Module
	Force	PT	Physical Training
MPF(F)	Maritime Pre-positioning	RAM	Rolling Airframe Missile
	Force (Future)	RB-M	Response Boat - Medium
MPS	Maritime Pre-positioning	RCB	Riverine Command Boat
	Squadron	RCOH	Refuelling and Complex
MSC	Military Sealift Command		Overhaul
MSST	Maritime Safety and	RCS	Rescue Capable System
	Security Team	RIMPAC	Rim of the Pacific
MSRT	Maritime Security Response	RMS	Remote Mine-hunting
	Team		System
MSU	Marine Safety Unit	Ro-Ro	Roll On - Roll Off
MSW	Main Seawater System	ROS	Reduced Operating Status
MT	Motor Tanker	ROV	Remotely Operated Vehicle
MV	Merchant Vessel	RRF	Ready Reserve Fleet
NAB	Naval Amphibious Base	SALM	Single Anchor Leg Moor
NAS	Naval Air Station	SB	Shipbuilder
NATO	North Atlantic Treaty	SBX	Sea-based X-Band Radar
	Organization	SCBA	Self-contained Breathing
NAVSEA	Naval Sea Systems		Apparatus
	Command	SCW	Seabee Combat Warfare
NAVSUP	Naval Supply Systems		Specialist Insignia
	Command	SDS	Submarine Decompression
NAWC	Naval Air Warfare Centre		System
NCWRON	Naval Coastal Warfare	SEAL	Sea Air and Land (USN
	Squadron		Special Forces)
NDAF	Naval Defence Logistics	SIGINT	Signals Intelligence
	Agency & Air Force Ships	SLBM	Submarine Launched
NDRF	National Defence Reserve		Ballistic Missile
	Force	SLEP	Service Life Extension
NECC	Navy Expeditionary Combat		Program
	Command	SRDRS	Submarine Rescue Diving
NIFC-CA	Naval Integrated Fire		and Compression System
	Control - Counter Air	SS	Steam Ship

SSN	Attack Submarine (Nuclear Powered)	T-ATF	Auxiliary Fleet Tug
SBN	Ballistic Missile Submarine (Nuclear Powered)	T-MLP	Auxiliary Mobile Landing Platform
SSC	Seabase to Shore Connector	TPSB	Transportable Port Security Boat
SSGN	Cruise Missile Submarine (Nuclear Powered)	UAV	Unmannned Air Vehicle
SSV	Submarine Support Vessel	USCG	US Coast Guard
SURTASS	Surface Towed Array System	USMC	US Marine Corps
SWAN	Shipboard Wide-Area Network	USN	United States Navy
SWATH	Small Waterplane Twin Hull	USNS	United States Naval Ship
TACAMO	Take Charge & Move Out	USS	United States Ship
TACTOM	Tactical Tomahawk	UTB	Utility Boat
T-ACS	Auxiliary Crane Ship	VAW	Airborne Early Warning Squadron
T-AFS	Auxiliary Combat Stores Ship	VAQ	Electronic Warfare Squadron
T-AGF	Auxiliary Command Ship	VBSS	Visit, Board, Search & Seizure
T-AGM	Auxiliary Range Instrumentation Ship	VFA	Fighter Attack Squadron
T-AGOR	Auxiliary Acoustic Survey Ship	VFC	Composite Fighter Squadron
T-AGOS	Auxiliary Ocean Surveillance Ship	VLS	Vertical Launch System
T-AGS	Auxiliary Oceonographic Survey Ship	VMA	USMC Attack Squadron
T-AH	Auxiliary Hospital Ship	VMAQ	USMC Electronic Warfare Squadron
T-AKE	Auxiliary Dry Cargo Ship	VMFA	USMC Fighter Attack Squadron
T-AK	Auxiliary Transport, Container	VMFA(AW)	USMC Fighter Attack Squadron (All Weather)
T-AKR	Auxiliary Transport, Ro-Ro	VMFT	USMC Fighter Training Squadron
T-AO	Auxiliary Fleet Replenishment Oiler	VMGR	USMC Tanker/Transport Squadron
T-AOT	Auxiliary Transport Tanker	VMM	USMC Tilt Rotor Squadron
T-AOE	Auxiliary Fast Combat Support Ship	VMU	USMC Unmanned Aerial Squadron
T-ARC	Auxiliary Cable Repair Ship	VOO	Vessel of Opportunity
T-AVB	Auxiliary Aviation Logistics Ship	VP	Maritime Patrol Squadron
		VTU	Volunteer Training Unit
		VQ	Special Warfare Squadron
T-ARS	Auxiliary Rescue and Salvage Ship	VR	Transport Squadron
		VRC	Composite Transport

	Squadron	WLIC	Inland Construction Tender
V/STOL	Vertical/Short Take-off or Landing	WLM	Coastal Buoy Tender
		WLR	River Buoy Tender
VT	Training Squadron	WMEC	Medium Endurance Cutter
VUP	Unmanned Maritime Patrol Squadron	WMSL	Maritime Security Cutter (Large)
VX	Trials Squadron	WPB	Patrol Boat
WAGB	Icebreaker	WPC	Patrol Boat Coastal
WHEC	High Endurance Cutter	WTD	Watertight Door
WLB	Seagoing Buoy Tender	WTGB	Icebreaking Tug
WLBB	Seagoing Buoy Tender Icebreaker	WYTL	Small Harbour Tug
		YPC	Yard Patrol Craft
WLI	Inland Buoy Tender		